Erin:

Wishing you all the "JOY" and happiness you may seek. God has helped you become the very special person you are. Someday you will share yourself with many.

Love & Friendship Forever

Ro—Sweeney 3-27-94

The
Spirituality
of the
Body

The Spirituality of the Body

BIOENERGETICS FOR GRACE AND HARMONY

Alexander Lowen, M.D.

MACMILLAN PUBLISHING COMPANY · NEW YORK
COLLIER MACMILLAN PUBLISHERS · LONDON

Macmillan Publishing Company
866 Third Avenue, New York, NY 10022
Collier Macmillan Canada, Inc.

Library of Congress Cataloging-in-Publication Data
Lowen, Alexander.
    The spirituality of the body: bioenergetics for grace and harmony/Alexander Lowen.
        p. cm.
    Includes bibliographical references.
    ISBN 0-02-575871-3
    1. Health.   2. Mind and body.   3. Bioenergetics.   I. Title.
RA776.5.L68   1990
613—dc20   89-37196   CIP

Macmillan books are available at special discounts for bulk purchases for sales promotions, premiums, fund-raising, or educational use. For details, contact:

Special Sales Director
Macmillan Publishing Company
866 Third Avenue
New York, NY 10022

10 9 8 7 6 5 4 3 2 1

Printed in the United States of America

To FREDERIC L. LOWEN,
a gentle man

Wise men read very sharply all your private history in your look and gait and behavior. The whole economy of nature is bent on expression. The telltale body is all tongues. Men are like Geneva watches with crystal faces which express the whole movement.

RALPH WALDO EMERSON

Contents

Preface

IN this book I shall attempt to uncover health's spiritual face. We shall see that the subjective feeling of health is one of aliveness and pleasure in the body, a feeling that increases at times to joyfulness. It is in such states that we feel a kinship with all living creatures and recognize our connection to the world. Pain, on the other hand, isolates us and cuts us off from others. When we are ill, our health is compromised not only by our symptoms but by the isolation they impose on us.

We shall also see that health is manifested objectively in the gracefulness of the body's movements, in a bodily radiance or glow (no wonder we speak of "glowing health"), and in the body's softness and warmth. The total absence of these qualities denotes death or a fatal illness. The softer and more pliable we are, the closer we are to health. As we become more rigid with age, we draw closer to death.

Aldous Huxley describes three forms of grace: animal grace, human grace, and spiritual grace.[1] As we have seen, spiritual grace involves a sense of connectedness to a higher order. Human grace is reflected in a person's behavior toward his fellow man; it can properly be described as graciousness. We are familiar with animal grace from watching free and wild creatures. For me, watching squirrels playing in the trees is an exciting experience. Few humans can hope to approach the gracefulness and sureness of their movements. The swift flight of swallows is also awe-inspiring. To one degree or another, all wild animals have this beautiful quality of gracefulness of movement. For humans, according to Huxley, animal grace comes when we open ourselves to the "virtue of the sun and the spirit of the air" instead of abusing our bodies and interfering with the workings of our innate animal intelligence.[2]

However, humans do not and perhaps cannot live on the same plane as wild animals, for the fullness of animal grace, according to Huxley, is reserved for them. Man's nature is such that he must live a self-conscious life in time. What this means, according to Huxley, is that "animal grace is no longer sufficient for the conduct of life and must be supplemented by deliberate choices between right and wrong."[3] We must grant the validity of Huxley's argument, but if animal grace is not sufficient for the conduct of human life, it may still be necessary. To put it differently, how can behavior truly be gracious if it lacks a foundation in the body's animal grace? When one deliberately adopts a gracious style without grounding it in bodily feelings of pleasure, such graciousness is no more than a facade erected to impress or deceive the world.

According to the Bible, prior to eating the forbidden fruit of the tree of knowledge, man lived in the Garden of Eden without self-consciousness, just like any other animal. He was innocent and knew the joy of living in a state of grace. Along with the knowledge of good and evil came the responsibility to make choices, and man lost his innocence and became self-conscious. The harmony that had existed between man and God, between man and nature, was destroyed. Instead of the bliss of ignorance, man now knew and experienced "dis-ease." Joseph Campbell places some of the responsibility for this loss of harmony on the Christian tradition, which separates the spirit from the flesh. "The Christian separation of matter and spirit, of the dynamism of life and the values of the spirit, of natural grace and supernatural grace, has really castrated nature."[4]

Behind the Christian tradition is the Judeo-Grecian belief in the superiority of the mind over the body. When mind and body are separated, spirituality becomes an intellectual phenomenon—a belief rather than a vital force—while the body becomes simply flesh, or a biochemical laboratory, as in modern medicine. The dispirited body is characterized by its relative unaliveness and lack of grace. Its movements tend to have a mechanical quality, since they are to a large degree determined by the mind or will. When the spirit moves the body, it quivers with excitement and bounds with enthusiasm, like a stream cascading down a mountainside, or flows quietly, like a wide and deep river in a plain. Life does not always flow smoothly, but when one has to push or drag one's self through the days, there is something seriously wrong in the body's dynamics that disposes the person to illness.

True gracefulness is not something that is learned; it is part of man's natural endowment as one of God's creatures. Once lost, however, it can only be recovered by reestablishing the body's spirituality. To do that, we need to understand both why and how it was lost. But since one can't recover a lost object unless one knows what it is, we will start with an investigation of the natural body, one in which movement, feeling, and thinking are integrated in graceful actions. We will study the body as a contained and self-maintained energetic system that is dependent on and constantly interacting with the environment for its survival. An energetic perspective will enable us to comprehend the true nature of bodily grace and spirituality without becoming mystical. This will lead to an exploration of the role of feeling in human grace. In the absence of feeling, movement becomes mechanical and ideas become abstractions. One can preach love to a broken-spirited person whose soul is full of hate, but such preaching is ineffective. If we can restore the integrity of his spirit, his love will shine forth. We will investigate some of the disturbances that break a person's spirit, diminish the body's gracefulness, and undermine its health. Focusing on grace as a criterion of health will enable us to understand many of the emotional problems that plague human beings and to develop the gracefulness that promotes health.

Spirit and matter are joined in the concept of grace. In theology, grace is defined as "the divine influence acting within the heart to regenerate, sanctify and keep it." It could also be defined as the divine spirit acting within the body. The divine spirit is experienced as the natural gracefulness of the body and in the graciousness of the person's attitude toward all of God's creatures. Grace is a state of holiness, of wholeness, of connection to life, and of unity with the divine. This state is also one of health, as we shall see.

1

The Concept of Grace and Spirituality

OUR striving for health can be effective only if we have a positive concept of health. Defining health as the absence of disease is a negative view because it sees the body as a mechanic might look at an automobile, the parts of which can be replaced without disturbing the machine. That is not true of any living organism and certainly not true of human beings. We have feelings, which no machine has; we move spontaneously, which no machine is able to do; and we are connected in a very deep way to other living organisms and to nature. Our spirituality derives from this sense of connection to a force or order greater than ourselves. It matters little what name we give it or whether we leave it nameless, as the Hebrews do.

If we accept that human beings are spiritual creatures, then we must also accept that health is related to spirituality. I am convinced that losing the sense of connection to other people, to animals, to nature, results in a serious disturbance of mental health. On a cultural level, we call this disturbance anomie. On an individual level, we describe it as a feeling of isolation, aloneness, and emptiness that can lead to depression or, in more severe cases, to schizoid withdrawal. It is not generally recognized that when connection with the outer world is broken there is a concomitant loss of connection with the bodily self. This lack of feeling of the body underlies both depression and the schizoid state. It is due to a reduction in the body's vitality, to a diminution of its vital spirit, to a decrease in its energetic state. Of course, mental health cannot be separated from physical health; true health includes both aspects of the personality. All the same, medicine has no valid physical or objective criteria for evaluating mental health. One can only measure mental health by the absence of disturbing elements in the patient's personality and by his complaints. Symptoms, we must realize, are subjective phenomena.

Objectively, mental health is reflected in the aliveness of the body that can be observed in the brightness of the eyes, the color and warmth of the skin, the spontaneity of expression, the vibrancy of the body, and the gracefulness of movement. The eyes are particularly important because they are windows to the soul. In them can be seen the life of the spirit. Where that spirit is absent—as in schizophrenia—the eyes are vacant. In the depressed state, the eyes are sad, and in many cases one can see a deep despair in the person. In the borderline personality the eyes are dull, indicating that the function of seeing—that is, seeing as understanding what one observes—is crippled. The dulling of the eyes can be traced in most cases to the experience of horror in childhood. Because the eyes are important in the way we relate to one another and to the world about us, I shall analyze their function more fully in chapter 9, "Face to the World." People with bright eyes tend to look at one another directly, to make eye contact that is a feeling connection with the other person. The bright color and warmth of the skin are due to the strong flow of blood to the surface of the body—from the heart, acting under the influence of the "divine" spirit. In the same way, the vibrancy of the body and the gracefulness of movement are manifestations of this spirit. We can only conclude that the Greeks were correct in saying that a healthy mind can only exist in a healthy body.

In view of the above, one may question whether it is meaningful and effective to treat mental illness without regard to the state of the body or to heal physical illness without any consideration for the state of the person's spirit. The answer to the above question must be both yes and no. Where the elimination of a distressing symptom is the goal of the treatment, an exclusive focus on the limited area of the person involved in the symptom is meaningful and can be effective. Almost all of medical practice is engaged in this kind of treatment. But such a practice does not restore the person to a whole state of health, nor does it act upon the underlying cause of the disorder; namely, the factors in the personality of an individual that predispose him to the disease. Now, it may not always be necessary to investigate this issue. If a person breaks a bone or if a cut becomes infected, one can act directly upon the injured area to promote its healing. Although this is a limited approach to illness, Western medicine has achieved some remarkable results in the treatment of disease. Though its attitude toward the body is mechanistic, its knowledge of the body's mechanism, structurally and biochemically, has enabled physicians to perform some seeming miracles. But this type of medicine has very definite limitations that many of its practitioners refuse to recognize. Many of the most common illnesses are resistant to this approach. Lower back trouble with or without sciatic nerve involvement is widespread among Western people, yet few orthopedic surgeons understand the illness and can effectively treat it. Arthritis and rheumatic disorders are similar ailments that defy medical science. The intractability of cancer is well known. My point is that these are diseases of the whole person and can only be understood in such terms. Understanding does not always lead to cure, but it is impossible to restore a person to true health without it.

I treated a woman some years ago who suffered from a severe intestinal disorder. She was allergic to many foods, including bread, sugar, and meat. Eating any food to which she was allergic would result in cramps and diarrhea, which could leave her weak and depleted. She lived, necessarily, on a very strict diet. Despite her care, she had attacks of diarrhea. She was underweight and undercharged energetically. Of course, she consulted many doctors. Their examinations revealed that her intestine was infected with parasites, both amoebic and fungal. Their medication, however, produced only short-lived relief. The parasites would seem to disappear, only to return again soon.

As her therapist, I came to know this woman well. I will call her Ruth. She was a petite woman, rather attractive in face and body. Two features stood out, however, as severe distortions. Her eyes were large and very frightened looking. She was also myopic. And her jaw was extremely tight and thrust forward. The expression of the jaw was very defiant, as if to say, "You won't destroy me." In view of the strong fear in her eyes, it could also say, "I won't be afraid of you." Ruth was not conscious of this strong fear.

The following information came out in the course of the analysis. Ruth was an only child of Jewish parents who had emigrated to this country shortly after the war and before Ruth was born. She recognized that both parents had emotional problems. Her mother was a frightened and anxious woman. Her father was sickly but hardworking. Ruth described her childhood as unhappy. She felt that her mother was hostile to her, burdening her with chores that left Ruth with no time to play. Her mother was also critical of her. Ruth could not remember any warmth or close physical contact with her mother. On the other hand, she retained some warm feelings toward her father, who she felt loved her. He, however, had distanced himself from her when she was still little.

Ruth's spirit was broken, but her body was not fully "dispirited." There was an emptiness in her body that indicated that her spirit was weak. She was not aggressive. She had great difficulty reaching out and taking in any good feeling. Her breathing was shallow, and her energy was low. She realized that she had a problem with reaching out that she attributed to her distrust of people. I related her intestinal trouble to this distrust and to the consequent inability to take and absorb nourishment. It was as if she had experienced her mother's milk as being poison. She had been nursed for a short time, and while she had no memory of being weaned, I regarded that event as the first major trauma of her life. Certainly her mother's hostility was poisonous. A second major trauma was the loss of the connection to her father due largely to the mother's jealousy over her father's love for her. His withdrawal left her helpless before a hostile mother and gave her the feeling that no one cared.

Despite my efforts to help her, Ruth was distrustful of me. Although she felt more alive after our sessions, the improvement did not hold. Then a remarkable thing happened. Ruth had a friend who told her about a woman who practiced Christian Science healing. Ruth consulted a number of times with this woman, who spoke to her about the healing power of faith in Jesus Christ. The woman explained to Ruth that the soul is immortal and that although the body may die the person lives on in his soul. She also pointed out that Ruth was identified with her symptoms. She could break this identification by realizing that the symptoms were part of her body, not of her soul. And then Ruth said to me, "Can you imagine. Me, a Jewish girl, believing in Jesus Christ."

The remarkable thing was that Ruth's symptoms had completely disappeared. She looked and felt good. Even eating food to which she was allergic caused no adverse reaction. It seemed like a miracle of faith, for faith can produce seeming miracles. I shall devote a later chapter to the subject of faith. However, one can offer an explanation for the apparent miracle of Ruth's recovery.

That explanation is based on the thesis that the symptoms and the pathological condition of Ruth's intestines represent her identification with her mother, whom Ruth saw as a deprived and suffering person. It is one of the peculiarities of human nature that this kind of identification is always made with the oppressor. As we saw, Ruth had been oppressed by her mother, was frightened of her, and hated her. At the same time, she felt terribly sorry for her and guilty. She was tied to her mother in her unconscious; that is, in her spirit. She had to suffer.

For a Jewish woman to accept Christ entails a break with her family and her past. By this action, Ruth released her spirit from its pathological bond to her mother's suffering and temporarily overcame her illness. In therapy, we describe such an event as a breakthrough. While a breakthrough is an important step in restoring health and freeing the spirit, it needs reinforcement. Indeed, following this experience, Ruth was more relaxed, but her face was still tense, her eyes still frightened, and her shoulders still held up. The logjam that held her spirit imprisoned was beginning to break up, but she knew she had more conflicts to resolve and more work to do with her body to regain her gracefulness.

Another patient who accomplished a breakthrough in therapy, freeing her spirit, was Barbara, a woman in her late fifties who had suffered for more than ten years from constant atacks of diarrhea. The ingestion of sugar or any sweetened food generally provoked an attack. Stress was also a factor, since the attacks occurred more frequently when she was away from home. Her greatest source of stress, however, was a second marriage in which there were many conflicts. Despite her difficulties, Barbara was reluctant to seek help, believing that she had to overcome her problems herself. When she started therapy, her progress was very slow. Barbara had to be in control of the therapy, just as she had to be in control in her life. Control meant holding in her feelings, dealing with every situation unemotionally. Losing control, letting feelings out, raised the specter of insanity.

Barbara's breakthrough occurred when she finally realized that she had failed. Her marriage was on the verge of breaking up, and she felt desperate. As she began to acknowledge these feelings, for the first time in many years, Barbara broke down and cried. She felt that she had lost and was lost. She had always been her daddy's "little girl," and she had always believed that she could please and hold her man. The loss of her first husband by death did not disturb this illusion. Following her crying session, Barbara felt strong anger toward her father for his betrayal of the implied promise to love her if she would be a "good" girl. To be a good girl meant to hold in her feelings and always be smart and strong. This attitude had seemed to work in her first marriage, in which she had been in control. It was not working in her second marriage, which increased her need for control. As a result, she had developed a spastic colon, which broke down under stress in episodes of diarrhea. After her breakthrough in therapy, Barbara no longer suffered these bouts, a fact she initially attributed to her care in avoiding sugar. Only after she had, on one occasion, indulged her desire for sweets with no ill effects did Barbara realize that she was free from her problem. This, too, was a spiritual healing, for in releasing her feelings, she released her spirit.

Ruth's case reveals the power of a spiritual force to heal the body. Christian Science is known for its belief in and use of this power in its healing program. However, Western medicine, because it has a mechanistic orientation, refuses to recognize this force, which is an essential element of Eastern medicine. In the East, the primary focus has been maintaining health rather than curing disease, a focus that requires the holistic view of health that is missing from Western medicine. Throughout the East, health is generally seen as a state of balance or harmony between the individual and the universal. This principle underlies the practice of t'ai chi ch'uan, which is a program of exercises aimed at promoting a sense of unity with the cosmos through movements that are flowing and graceful. The same principle is operative in meditation, which seeks to still the mind so that the individual can sense his inner spirit and feel its connection with the universal spirit. The concept of balance and harmony also applies to the two great forces the Chinese call *yin* and *yang*. These two forces, one representing the earth and the other the sky, should be balanced in the individual as they are in the universe. Illness is seen as an imbalance between them.

It is possible to understand the illnesses of Ruth and Barbara in terms of an imbalance of forces. The two forces involved can be equated with the ego and the body, thinking and feeling, good and bad. In both cases that imbalance was evident in the domination of the head over the body. For Ruth, to be good meant to be sensitive to her mother's suffering and to deny her own needs. For Barbara, to be good meant to be smart and strong; to be bad meant to be emotional. Throughout this book I shall emphasize the need for harmony between the ego and the body as the basis for gracefulness and true spirituality.

It is important to realize that Eastern and Western philosophies and religions look at spirituality—or one's sense of connection to a higher order—from different points of view. Whereas Eastern thinking sees spirituality as a bodily phenomenon, Western thinking views it primarily as a function of the mind. Another way of expressing the difference is to say that in the West spirituality is largely a matter of belief, while in the East it is more a matter of feeling. It is true, of course, that belief can affect feelings just as feelings can determine beliefs. In Ruth's story we saw how a belief in Christ and the immortality of the soul can greatly influence bodily processes. On the other hand, a transcendental experience in which one feels the strength of the spirit can lead to or support a belief in a divinity. Nevertheless, we must recognize that there is or has been a fundamental difference in the two views of man's relation to his world. The East has always manifested a greater respect for nature than the West, believing that man's well-being depends on harmony with nature. The Tao is the way of nature. The West, at least in the last centuries, has aimed at power and control over nature, a difference that is reflected in Western attitudes toward the body. Western man thinks of bodily health in terms of fitness, to use a current expression— fitness for the work of life in the same way that a machine is fit to do a job. The exercises he does, lifting weights or working out with machines, denote this attitude. In contrast, Eastern exercises such as yoga or tai chi ch'uan reflect a person's interest in the aliveness or spiritual quality of the body.

The story of the fall from grace is repeated with the birth of each new individual. Like every other mammal, a human

baby is born into a state of animal grace, although for some
months his movements are awkward. He does not yet have the
muscular coordination that will enable him to move easily to
satisfy his needs. Even the graceful deer struggles awkwardly
to stand on its legs when it is first born. But no animal organism
needs to make a conscious effort to develop coordination,
which is genetically programmed to develop as growth occurs.

Even in its earliest months an infant makes some movements that are truly graceful. The most evident is in the action
of reaching out with its mouth and lips to suck its mother's
breast. There is a softness, a sweetness, and a flowing quality
to this movement that reminds one of a flower opening its
petals to the morning sun. The mouth is the first area of the
baby's body to mature; its sucking action is essential to life. In
contrast, so many adults that I have seen and worked with
cannot reach out with their lips freely and fully. In many the
lips are tight and hard, the jaws tense and grim. Some even
have difficulty opening their mouths wide. Within a few
months after birth a baby can reach an arm out to touch the
mother's body in a soft, gentle motion that is very graceful.

Sooner or later, however, in the process of growing up,
children fall from grace as they are forced to conform to external expectations rather than follow their internal impulses.
When their own impulses go against parental injunctions, children are quickly taught that such behavior is bad. If the behavior is persisted in, the child himself is labeled bad. In almost
all cases the impulses and behavior of very young children are
innocent; the child is simply being true to his own nature. A
common example is the child who is tired and wishes to be
picked up and carried. But his mother may be tired herself,
busy, or carrying a heavy package that prevents her from picking up the child. The result is a crying child who exasperates
his mother by refusing to walk. Some mothers will castigate the

child and tell him to stop crying. If his irritating behavior persists, the mother may hit him, which only causes more tears. So far in this illustration the child has not lost its gracefulness because it has not yet suppressed its impulses. As long as a child can cry fully, its body will remain soft. Babies often experience frustrations and pain that cause their little bodies to stiffen and tighten. But the tightness and tension don't hold. Quickly the chin begins to tremble, and the child bursts into sobs. As waves of crying pass through the child's body, its stiffness and rigidity melt. But there comes a time when it is reprimanded for crying, when it must choke back its sobs and swallow its tears. It is at this point that the child is pushed out of its state of grace to become an individual who is no longer free to "follow its bliss," as Joseph Campbell recommended.

Another natural feeling that is not acceptable to many parents is anger, especially when it is directed at them. But children will spontaneously strike out at parents when they feel constrained and imposed upon. Few parents will accept a child's anger, because it threatens their power and control. In one way or another, they will teach the child that such behavior is bad and will be punished. Even such innocent activities as running, making noise, and being active can irritate some parents, who will demand that the child quiet down, behave, and sit still.

For many children, the list of dos and don'ts is quite extensive. Obviously, some parental control is needed to raise children, but too often the issue is not what is best for the child but what is best for the parent. Very often the conflict becomes a power struggle. No matter who wins in this type of conflict, both parties lose. Whether the child submits or rebels, the loving connection between parent and child is broken. With the loss of love, the spirituality of the child is damaged, and he falls from grace.

The loss of grace is a physical phenomenon. We see it in the way people move and stand. Quite often I will see a patient in consultation for the fairly common complaint of depression. As I pointed out in a previous study,[1] depression affects not only a person's thinking but his movements, appetites, breathing, and energy production. To fully understand the disease, I look at the body. Very often I find the person standing in the position of a good boy or girl waiting to be told what to do. This unconscious attitude has become ingrained in the personality by becoming structured in the body. When I point out the meaning of this stance to patients, they invariably confirm that they were regarded as good children by their parents. Such "good" children grow up to be productive workers, but they will never be vitally alive or graceful unless there is a radical transformation in their personalities.

It is often said that we are shaped by our experience, but when I make this statement, I mean it quite literally. Our bodies reflect our experiences. To illustrate this concept, I will describe three cases from my experience. The first concerns a Dutch psychologist who participated in a workshop that I ran at the Esalen Institute many years ago. In what has now become routine bioenergetic practice, it is my custom to look at a person's body for clues to his experience. This person's body showed an unusual disturbance: a six-inch-deep indentation in the left side of his body. I had never seen such an indentation before and could make no sense of it. When I questioned him about its occurrence, he related that it had begun as a very slight concavity on the left side of his body when he was eleven years old. Over three years it had deepened to the point where it was when I saw him. He had never consulted a doctor about it because it had never interfered with his normal functioning. I asked him whether anything unusual had happened in his life when he was eleven years old. He answered that his mother had remarried and he was sent away to boarding school. That statement seemed to make no impression on the rest of the group, but it struck me as significant. I immediately saw the meaning of his indentation. It was as if a hand had forcefully pushed him aside.

The second case is that of a young man who had the broadest shoulders I have ever seen in a man. When I commented on this during his consultation, he spoke of his father, describing him as a man whom he greatly admired. He said that once when he came home from military school at the age of sixteen, his father had asked him to stand beside him in front of a mirror. The young man saw that he was as tall as his father and was forcibly struck by the thought that if he grew any taller he would look down on him. From that day on, he did not gain any height, but his shoulders broadened. It was evident to me that the energy of growth was directed sideways to save the son from surpassing his father.

The third example is the case of a young man who was quite tall, about six feet three inches. He complained of feeling cut off from life. He said that when he walked he did not feel the lower part of his legs and his feet. As he took a step, he could not sense when his foot would hit the ground.[2] His growth had occurred rather rapidly when he was about fourteen years old. When I questioned him about his life, he related that his father had moved out of the parental bedroom and taken over the boy's bedroom at that time. He, in turn, was forced to sleep in the garret. He felt, he said, that he had been "kicked upstairs."

These emotional traumas may not seem severe enough to most people to cause such noticeable distortions in the body. It is my experience, however, that the depth and intensity of a person's feelings are most often expressed in bodily reactions. Every experience a person lives through affects his body and is

recorded in his mind. If the experience is pleasurable, it furthers the health, vitality, and grace of the body. The opposite
is true for those painful experiences that are negative. The
effect may be temporary if the individual can react appropriately to the trauma, since the body can and does heal itself.
However, if the reaction is blocked, the trauma leaves a mark
on the body in the form of chronic muscular tension.

Consider what happens to the child who is taught that
crying is not acceptable. The impulse to cry resides in the body
and has to be blocked somehow from expression. To control
that impulse, the muscles involved in crying must contract and
stay contracted until the impulse fades away. But the impulse
doesn't die out. Instead, it retreats to the interior of the body,
where it lives on in the unconscious. It can be reactivated years
later through therapy or some powerful life experience. Until
that happens, the relevant musculature—in this case, the muscles of the mouth, jaw and throat—will be in a state of chronic
tension. That this problem is very common is evident by the
number of people who suffer from tense jaws, which in its
severe form is called TMJ (temporomandibular joint syndrome).

Wherever there is chronic muscular tension in the body,
natural impulses are unconsciously blocked. A good example is
the case of a man whose shoulder muscles were so tight and
contracted that he could not raise his arms above his head. The
block represented an inhibition against raising a hand to *the
parent.* When I asked this man if he had ever been able to be
angry with his father, he replied no. The idea that he could hit
his father was as unacceptable to him as it had been to his
father. But the consequence of this inhibition was to destroy
the natural gracefulness of his arm movements.

When I was in Japan a number of years ago, I witnessed a
child of about three beating his mother with his fists. I was

impressed by the fact that the mother did nothing to stop the child or to retaliate in any way. I learned later that teaching a child the control necessary to develop social graces does not begin until the child is six years old. Prior to the age of six a child is regarded as innocent, without knowledge of right or wrong. At six a child's ego is developed enough that learning is a conscious activity, based on desire, not fear. At that point a child is considered old enough to consciously model his behavior on his parents'. Failure to learn is not punished by physical force or the withdrawal of love but by shaming the child. Schooling, too, generally begins at that age. In our culture, there is a strong tendency to start the process earlier.[3] Children do learn before the age of six, but their learning is entirely spontaneous. Imposing so many rules and regulations before that age operates to restrict and limit a child's aliveness, spontaneity, and gracefulness.

The capacity of the Japanese and other Eastern people to see the child as innocent stems from a deep respect for nature. If we live in harmony with nature and with ourselves, we can live in harmony with our children. Western people, on the other hand, seek to subordinate nature. If we exploit nature, we will inevitably exploit our children.

Yet Oriental people are becoming Westernized as their economy industrializes. An industrial society is based on power, which starts off as the power to *do* but ends as the power to *control*. With power, man's relationship to nature changes. Control replaces the idea of harmony, and exploitation replaces respect. To have power and at the same time to strive for harmony is contradictory. Inevitably, Eastern people will suffer the same emotional disturbances that plague Western man: anxiety, depression, and the loss of gracefulness.

Unfortunately, one cannot return to the old ways. Innocence lost can never be regained. For this reason, the age-old practices of Eastern philosophers cannot resolve the emotional problems we face today. No amount of meditation will enable an individual to cry when his impulse to cry has been suppressed. No yoga exercise can release the tension in the shoulders of a man who dares not raise his hand in anger against an authority figure. This is not to say that the practice of meditation or yoga has no beneficial effect. There are many practices and exercises that have a positive value for one's health. Massage, for example, is both pleasurable and beneficial. Dancing, swimming, and walking are all exercises I highly recommend. But to restore gracefulness, one must know how it was lost. In the final analysis this is an analytic undertaking.

My focus on the body should make it clear that when I talk about analysis I am not talking about psychoanalysis. One does not regain gracefulness by lying on a couch or sitting in a chair and talking about one's life experiences. Such talk is necessary and helpful, but the chronic muscular tensions that accompany a loss of grace must be confronted on a bodily level. Bioenergetics, an approach I have been developing for the past thirty-five years, does just that. It is an approach that integrates Eastern and Western views and uses the power of the mind to understand the tensions that bind the body. It also mobilizes the body's energy to eliminate these tensions.

The unifying thread is the concept of energy, which pervades both Eastern and Western thinking. Energy is the force behind the spirit and therefore the basis for the body's spirituality. Consciously used, it becomes power. In the next chapter we will examine Eastern and Western concepts of energy and show how bioenergetics integrates the two positions.

2
The Energetic Concept

IT is characteristic of Eastern religious thinking to associate the spirit or spirituality with an energetic view of the body. Hatha-yoga, for example, postulates the existence of two opposing energies; ha, or sun energy, and tha, or moon energy. The goal of hatha-yoga is to achieve balance between these two forces. According to Yesudian and Haich, authors of *Yoga and Health*, "Our body is entwined by positive and negative currents, and when these currents are in complete equilibrium, we enjoy perfect health."[1] It is easy to understand why *primitive* people would regard the sun and the moon as energetic bodies, for both exert direct influence on the earth and its life. In Chinese thinking, health also depends on a proper balance between opposing energies, namely, yin and yang, representing earth energy and sky energy. The Chinese medical practice of acupuncture recognizes established channels through which these energies flow. By using needles or by applying pressure at selected points, the flow of energy in the body can be directed to cure disease and promote health.

Another way the Chinese mobilize the body's energy for health is through a program of special exercises known as t'ai chi ch'uan. T'ai chi movements are usually performed slowly and rhythmically, using only the minimum strength required to assume each position. According to Herman Kanz, "the emphasis is upon relaxation," which "aids the flow of internal energy called *chi* in Chinese or *ri* in Japanese. A reservoir of this energy is said to be in the lower abdominal area."[2] I will refer later in this book to other aspects of Eastern thinking about the flow of the body's energy.

Western thinking sees energy mostly in measurable, mechanistic terms. Because no instrument has been able to measure any of the energies taken for granted in the East, the Western scientific mind refuses to acknowledge their existence. Nevertheless, living organisms respond to aspects of the body's energy in ways that machines cannot. For example, the excitement that a lover feels when meeting his beloved is an energetic phenomenon to which no instrument is sensitive. The glow of a person in love with life itself is another energetic phenomenon that no instrument has yet recorded. (Although Kirlian photography has demonstrated the existence of an aura or glow about parts of the body, no one has yet succeeded in quantifying this phenomenon.)

Even before the recent infusion of Eastern thinking into Western culture, some people have questioned the view that the body is only a complex biochemical machine enlivened by a nebulous spirit and ennobled by a metaphysical soul. In fact, in the nineteenth century, French writer and philosopher Henri Bergson postulated the existence of a vital force or energy, called the *élan vital,* that animated the body. Exponents of vitalism, as this view came to be called, could not accept the notion that the functioning of a living organism could be fully explained in mechanical or chemical terms. But as the methods and techniques of scientific investigation developed, making it possible to show a biochemical basis for almost all actions of the body, vitalism came to be seen as a metaphysical concept beyond scientific investigation having no objective reality.

Modern medicine still subscribes to such a view. When I went to medical school at the age of thirty-six, I had been a student of Wilhelm Reich's and a therapist for some years. I wanted to know about the body and its illnesses, but I also wanted to understand it in human terms. More specifically, I wondered what role feelings play in health and illness and how we can explain love, courage, dignity, and beauty. The knowledge I gained in medical school has proved invaluable; unfortunately, no mention of these terms was ever made. Nor was there any reference to them in the medical textbooks. Even the important emotions of fear, anger, and sadness were not discussed, because they were regarded as psychological rather than physical. Pain was examined from neurological and biochemical points of view, but pleasure was beyond investigation, even though it is such a powerful force in our lives.

The most important vacuum in medical education then and even now, to a slightly lesser degree, is human sexuality. Yet as every doctor knows, this is a function of great importance in the life and health of people. The reproductive function was treated fully, but sexuality was ignored for the reason that it is not limited to an organ but involves feelings that embrace the whole body. We shall see that through the study of this function Reich arrived at some understanding of the energetic factor in the living process.

Medical science, as we know it, is primarily concerned with organ functions. Doctors necessarily specialize in treating different systems, such as the respiratory, circulatory, or digestive systems. A science of the whole person is unknown in Western medicine. One might think it to be the domain of psychiatry or psychology, but these disciplines have limited themselves to the study of mental processes and their influence on the body.

The view that mental processes belong to one domain, psychology, while physical processes belong to another, organic medicine, denies the essential unity or wholeness of an individual. Such a view is the result of dissociating the spirit from the body and limiting it to the mind. This split has emasculated psychiatry and sterilized medicine. We can overcome this disruption of man's unity only by returning the psyche to the body. It was originally there, for *Funk and Wagnall's International Dictionary* says that *psyche* in its original meaning was "the vital principle which activates the inner springs of action and development." Only later did it represent "the spiritual being as distinct from the body." Its connection to the body is also shown by its root, *psychein,* which means to breathe. A holistic view of the organism would recognize that the body is imbued with a spirit that is activated by its psyche and mindful of its actions.

Since psyche as defined above is a vitalistic concept, science could not accept it and it was therefore relegated to the realm of metaphysics. Yet it was through psychology in the form of psychoanalysis that the way was opened to an understanding of spirit as an energetic phenomenon. That way led into the territory of sexuality, which traditional medicine had ignored. Freud came face-to-face with sexuality in his attempt to understand the hysterical symptom, a physical illness that could not be explained by medical science and for which there was no valid psychological explanation until Freud published his clas-

sic study. He showed that hysteria was the result of the transference on to the physical plane of a psychic conflict about
sexuality that stemmed from an early traumatic sexual experience. But how this transference occurred neither Freud nor the
other psychoanalysts could explain. The result is that psychosomatic medicine is bedeviled by the split between psyche and
soma and cannot connect the two.

That connection was made by Reich through the use of an
energetic concept. He realized that the conflict occurred on
both levels, psychic and somatic, at the same time. He saw
psyche and soma as two aspects of a unitary process, one
mental and the other physical, much like the head and tail
faces of a coin. Whatever one does with the coin affects both
sides simultaneously. But mind and body are also different
functions that act upon and influence each other. He formu-
lated his conceptualization as the principle of psychosomatic
unity and antithesis. Unity exists on an energetic level in the
depths of the organism; on the phenomenal level there is
antithesis or opposition. This seemingly complex relationship
can be clearly shown by dialectical diagram (fig. 2.1).

The question that immediately arises concerns the nature of
this energetic process and of the energy involved. Reich saw
the energy process as a pulsation (expansion and contraction,
as in the beating of the heart) and the propagation of waves
of excitation that can be experienced as streamings in the body.
But the idea of an energy at work in the body specifically in
the sexual function was Freud's. He recognized that other
physical ailments, like neurasthenia, hypochondriasis, and anxiety were related to a disturbance of the sexual function. Since
the sexual act ends in an emotional discharge, Freud realized
that the discharge was energetic in nature and postulated that
the sexual drive was activated by the buildup of sexual energy,
which he called *libido*. Freud originally believed that libido was

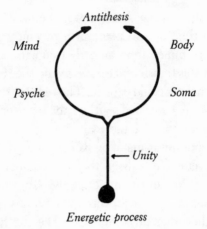

Figure 2.1. Reich's view of the mind and body, unified at
a deep level, but on a more superficial level, opposed.

a physical energy, but unable to prove its existence, he later
defined it as the mental energy of the sexual drive. In so doing,
he increased the split between mind and body.

Unlike Freud, Jung saw the libido as the energetic force that
activates all bodily movements and functions. He stopped
short, however, of calling it a physical force. This left the spirit,
the psyche, and the libido as metaphysical concepts and spirituality as a mental phenomenon.

Reich took Freud's original concept of the libido as a physical energy and performed some experiments to show that it
could be measured. He demonstrated that the electrical charge
at the surface of an erogenous zone (the lips, the nipples, and
the palms of the hand) increased when the area was pleasurably
stimulated. Painful stimulation, on the other hand, served to
decrease the charge. In addition, Reich also showed that plea-

surable excitation was associated with an increased flow of blood to the excited area and that painful stimulation was associated with some withdrawal of body fluid.³

These experiments allowed Reich to resolve the conflict between the vitalists and the mechanists. The link between tumescence, increased charge, and pleasurable stimulation does not occur in inanimate nature. Yet, he pointed out, "living matter does function on the basis of the same physical laws as non-living matter."⁴ The laws simply operate differently, since the living body is a self-contained energy system.

Later, however, Reich believed that a special energy was involved in the living process. He called this energy *orgone* and claimed that it was the primordial energy of the universe. During the years that I was associated with Reich, I, too, believed in the existence of this energy. In my opinion, there is some evidence to support the idea that the energy of the living process is other than electromagnetism. We can agree that it takes energy to drive the wheels of life. To avoid the arguments that would arise through the use of the term *orgone* or any similar name, I use the term *bioenergy* to refer to the energy of life. Since my form of treatment is based on an understanding of the energetic processes in the body, I call it bioenergetic analysis.

I will digress here to explain bioenergetic analysis so that the reader can more easily understand what follows. In bioenergetic analysis the personality is seen as a pyramidal structure. At the top or head is the mind and the ego. At the base, or on the deepest body level, are the energetic processes that activate the person. These processes result in movements that lead to feelings and end in thoughts. The relationship between these elements is shown in figure 2.2.

Broken lines between the different levels of the personality indicate the interrelationship of these different layers. In bio-

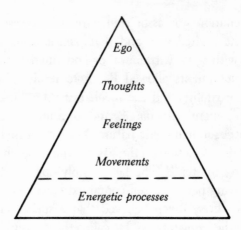

Figure 2.2. The hierarchy of the personality.

energetic analysis each level is studied to understand the personality. Because of their critical importance at the base of the pyramid the energetic processes are an area of major focus. How much energy a person has and how he uses his energy are subject to constant evaluation.

We know that energy is produced in the body by the chemical reactions involved in the metabolism of food. Although the chemistry of metabolism is quite complex, in essence it is similar to the process whereby fuel is converted into energy. F (fuel or food) $+ O_2 \rightarrow CO_2 + E$ (energy). What distinguishes living organisms from inanimate nature is that this process is contained within a membrane so that the energy produced is not lost to the environment but used by the organism to promote its life functions. One of its main functions is to obtain from the environment the ingredients necessary to perpetuate the production of energy. This requires that the membrane be permeable to food and oxygen coming in and to the waste products of metabolism going out. For organisms more complicated than bacteria or simple one-celled animals, this process involves actively searching for necessary supplies. An organism's movements cannot be purely random, therefore. They must be guided by some sensitivity to the environment. One of the foremost students of the functioning of protoplasm remarked, "Protoplasm may not be intelligent but it does the intelligent thing."[5] The intelligent thing is to open up and reach out for food, love, and pleasurable contacts and to withdraw from danger or pain. However, the process is not a mechanical one; every organism is constantly probing and testing its environment. This reaching out and pulling back is part of a pulsatory activity within the organism that includes the beating of the heart, the rise and fall of the lungs, and the peristaltic action of the digestive tract. All of these are caused by a state of excitement in every cell and every organ of the body. Life can thus be defined as a state of contained excitement in which energy is produced that drives the internal processes that sustain the life functions as well as the external actions that maintain or increase the organism's excitement.

We start life with a high potential for excitability that gradually diminishes as we get older. I believe the explanation for the loss of excitability with age is that the body becomes more structured—and more rigid—with time. Eventually, an older person becomes so set in his ways that he can barely move at all. I cannot recall ever seeing an older person jump for joy the way a young child can. Infants have the most spirited bodies of all, because they are far more sensitive than the rest of us to their environment and to the people around them. Yet the elderly are more consciously spiritual, for they are far more aware of their connectedness to the world around them. The concept of the spirituality of the body includes a compelling spirit plus a strong awareness of spiritual connectedness.

The process of making connections with the outside world

is an energetic process. To picture the way it occurs between two people, consider two tuning forks tuned to the same frequency. When they are close to one another, striking one tuning fork sets the other into motion. A similar concept explains the connection between two people deeply in love. The image of two hearts that beat as one may not be pure metaphor. As we have seen, our hearts and bodies are pulsatory systems that promulgate waves—waves that can affect other bodies and hearts. A mother's ability to sense what is going on in her infant depends on this kind of connection between them.

A sense of connection with the universal can be achieved by losing one's sense of self either by surrendering it or transcending it. The sense of self—also called the ego—is the boundary that creates an individual self. Enclosed within its boundaries is a self-maintaining energy system whose essential feature is its state of excitement. In figures 2.3A–C, the organism is shown as a circle enclosing a pulsating energy core. Without a boundary, neither self nor consciousness would exist.

Figure 2.3A shows the normal energetic interaction of an organism with its environment experiencing pleasure or pain. The ego mediates this interaction in the interest of self-preservation (when the organism encounters painful stimuli) or fulfillment (when the organism encounters pleasurable stimuli).

Figure 2.3B shows how waves of excitation from the core pass out into the world when the ego is surrendered. At this point, the self is no longer separate. Such an experience, which can be achieved by deep meditation, results in a calm and peaceful state.

In Figure 2.3C, the inner excitation becomes so strong that the waves it promulgates—as in orgasm or any type of joyous excitation—overwhelm the ego, radiating out past the self-boundary. A feeling of unity with the cosmos is experienced, but the feeling is not one of peace but of ecstasy.

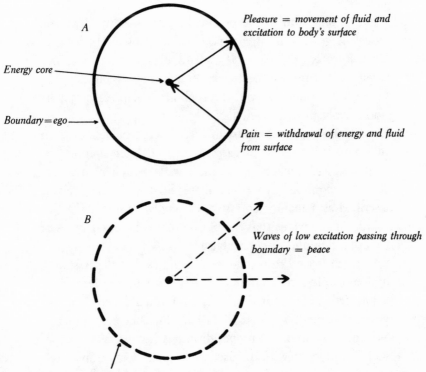

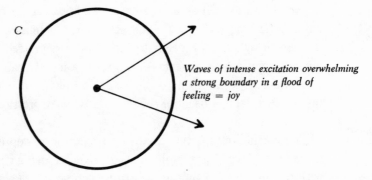

Figure 2.3. Energetic processes in the body.
(A) The normal reaction to pleasure and pain.
(B) The energetic process when the ego is surrendered.
(C) The energetic process when excitation is heightened.

Let us now turn to the practical aspects of this discussion about energy. The most common health problem of people in our culture is depression. It is hard to gauge its incidence because there are no objective criteria for depression except in its severest form. A person who is clinically depressed may lie motionlessly in bed or sit listlessly in a chair, expressing no desire to take an active part in life. A sense of despair is an important feature in some cases. In others, depression may be combined with anxiety or alternate with periods of hyperactivity. When mood swings dominate the picture, the illness is described as a manic-depressive, or bipolar, disorder. In this disorder it is obvious that the person moves between states of overexcitation and underexcitation.

While it is easy to recognize a severe case of depression, a mild case often goes unnoticed. A person may complain of being tired, and may attribute his diminished desire—another symptom of depression—to his fatigue. But if he gets more rest and still feels tired, the proper diagnosis is depression. As patients get in touch with themselves through therapy, one often hears them remark, "I realize I've been somewhat depressed most of my life." How did they fail to be aware of it? The answer is simple. They kept themselves busy. Many of my patients have admitted that their activity is a defense against depression; when they begin to feel a little depressed, they embark upon a new project. An interesting activity can serve to excite a person both psychologically and physically so that his energy level will rise, but sooner or later his depression will return.

The specific trauma that predisposes a person to depression is the loss of love.[6] An infant who is deprived of loving contact with his mother or a mother substitute can go into a state of anaclitic depression and die. Young or old, we all need some loving connection to sustain the excitability of our bodies.

Older people who lose a loved companion often lose the desire
to live. Most adults are able to reach out to many different
people for a feeling of connectedness, but the very young and
the very old are limited in their ability to establish loving ties.
All the same, the feeling of being connected is absolutely vital
to their health.

Even before birth, the human child is closely connected to
his mother. In the womb, that connection is the most physically intimate possible. Once born, an infant seeks to duplicate
that warmth at his mother's breast or in her arms. These
connections are vitally important to a baby. By exciting the
body, they stimulate its respiration and digestive functions.
Throughout life pleasurable physical intimacy continues to
have a positive effect, renewing an individual's enthusiasm and
life force.

The loss of a loving connection is often experienced as a
feeling of heartbreak or a painful constriction in the chest. All
but the very young can rebound from such a loss and relieve
the contraction by grieving or mourning the loss. The mourning process involves crying or wailing, which breaks the grip of
the contraction and restores the body to a more fluid condition.
As the heart's pulsations become strong again, waves of excitation reach and extend beyond the surface of the body. By
exciting other bodies, such waves serve to establish an energetic
connection between them.

Unfortunately, young children who suffer a loss of love cannot rebound from its effects until a new loving connection is
made. The release that crying affords is only temporary if a
connection to a loving figure is not reestablished. A young child
needs such a connection to maintain the strength of the pulsation within his body. Most often, the loss of love is not due to
the death or disappearance of the mother but to her inability
to meet the child's continuing demand for love. The mother

may have been a deprived child herself who suffered the loss
of her own mother's love. A vital, healthy father may be able
to respond to the child's need, but he is not a fully adequate
substitute, although he can assuage the pain of heartbreak. In
most cases, however, a child's heartbreak at the loss of his
mother's love persists into adulthood as a chronic contraction
in the chest that restricts breathing. By diminishing the supply
of available oxygen, such chronic tension dampens the metabolic fires and reduces the individual's production of energy.

An individual cannot raise his energy level simply by increasing his intake of food and/or oxygen. Unless there is a demand
by the body for this extra energy, the food will be stored as fat,
and the excess oxygen will result in a condition of hyperventilation. Organisms must maintain a balance between charge and
discharge, energy production and energy use. Demand controls
the equation between charge and discharge. Increasing an individual's basic energy level can only be done by making the body
more alive through the expression of feeling. A lack of aliveness
is always the result of suppressing feelings.

One of the surprising effects of diminished energy is increased activity, usually in an attempt to earn love. Most children who have suffered a loss of love believe that their loss is
due to a failure on their part to be lovable. Many mothers instill
this guilt by blaming the child for being too demanding, too
alive, too disobedient, too unhappy, too much. The child soon
realizes that he has to conform to his mother's demands if he
is to get any love. This conviction that love has to be earned
usually persists into adulthood, where it is often manifested in
the drive to achieve and the need for success. Such behavior
is typical of the type A personality, who is characterized by an
exaggerated drive to prove his worth coupled with a suppressed
anger manifested in constant irritability. Type A behavior is a
major factor predisposing an individual to depression or heart

disease.[7] But such behavior is also largely responsible for the chronic tiredness endemic to our culture.

Unfortunately, most people do not stop to feel their tiredness. Faced with the pressures of life, they believe that it is a matter of survival to go on as they have been. Feeling tired raises a deep fear that they may not be able to continue the struggle. Many find it difficult to say, "I can't." As children, they were taught that where there's a will, there's a way. To say, "I can't," is to admit failure, which is seen as evidence that they are unworthy of love.

There is also a physical reason for increased activity when one's spirits or energy is low. While it is possible to gain energy by relaxing, it is impossible to relax when one's energy is too low, since it takes energy to release muscular tension. This fact, which is generally unrecognized, can easily be illustrated and explained

When a muscle contracts, it performs work that consumes energy. In its contracted state, it can do no more work. To expand the muscle so that it becomes capable of further action requires that energy be produced by the muscle's cells. This, in turn, requires the introduction of oxygen and the removal of lactic acid. Figure 2.4 illustrates this principle of muscular action.

Consider an expanded muscle as one in which a spring has been stretched. It is now energetically charged. As a muscle contracts to perform work, it shortens and becomes harder. As the energy is used up, the spring is discharged. It recovers and relaxes by increasing its energetic charge, which stretches the spring again so it can do more work.

When a person is overtired and his energy is low, he can easily get wound up, just like a manic-depressive whose hyperexcitability and hyperactivity herald the onset of depression. The clearest example of this state of affairs is the agitated and

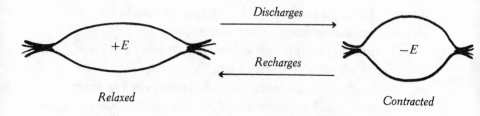

Figure 2.4. Energy in a muscle. The relaxed muscle is energetically charged and expanded, while the contracted muscle, having used up its energy in work, is compressed.

restless child who, despite his overtiredness, cannot quiet down
or sleep. Finally, in desperation, his parents may shout at him
or even shake him to quiet him down. The child reacts by
bursting into sobs, to which the parents respond by holding
and soothing him. After a good cry he falls asleep. The crying
has the effect of deepening the child's breathing, which provides energy for him to relax.

A high-energy person does not easily become overexcited
because his body, by virtue of its relaxed musculature, has the
capacity to hold or contain a high charge. Consequently, his
movements are slow, easy, and graceful. Like a high-powered
automobile that easily climbs a hill, an energized person moves
through life with a minimum of effort. Only in an emergency
will the fact that he is trying at all became apparent, but even
then he has enough energy in reserve to make it look easy.

Other aspects of the body reflect its energy charge as well.
Perhaps no feature is more indicative of the body's aliveness
than the eyes. The eyes have been described as windows of the
soul, but they are also windows of the body. As such, they
reveal an individual's inner flame. When that fire is hot, the
flame is bright and shines through the eyes. For example, when

a person is in love, his eyes shine, reflecting his highly charged state. The eyes also reveal feelings. Eyes sparkle when a person is joyful, glow when he is happy, and lose their luster when he is depressed. The eyes are so important in the life of a person that we shall devote a whole section to them later in this book.

The skin's quality is another sign of the body's degree of aliveness. Whether they are dark or light-skinned, high-energy people generally have pink or rosy skin tones, because their skin is suffused with blood. This suffusion results when a wave of excitation from the center of the person reaches the surface, producing a high-energy charge on the skin. A gray, white, yellow, or brownish skin tone indicates that the surface of the body is undercharged and that the circulation to the skin has been diminished. Similarly, rough, dry, or cold skin is a sign of a disturbance on both the circulatory and the energetic levels. These conditions also have emotional significance. In fear, for example, the blood is withdrawn from the surface, leaving the skin white, cold, and even clammy. Gooseflesh, another sign of fear, occurs when the elastic fibers of the skin contract, causing the follicles of the hair to stand out.

The body is shaped by its experience. The skin you love to touch was touched lovingly in infancy. The body's response to a loving touch is to expand with pleasurable excitement. In the absence of loving contact, a baby's body will shrink and become cold. Its excitability is diminished, its inner pulsation reduced. In a healthy person, that pulsation is strong and consistent, inspiring him to reach out and make loving contact with everyone and everything in his environment. Such a loving person is rare in our culture, which fails to see the spirituality inherent in the body's urge to reach out. The awareness questionnaire that follows will help you evaluate your own energy state and make you more conscious of how you function. How would you rate your energy level—high or low?

Awareness Questionnaire

Low-energy indicators:

a. Do you feel tired?
b. Do you have trouble getting up in the morning? Do you feel tired when you do get up?
c. Do you feel harried, driven, or continually pressured?
d. Are you always on the go?
e. Is it difficult for you to relax, to sit quietly?
f. Do you move slowly and easily, or are your movements quick and hurried?
g. Do you have trouble falling asleep?
h. Do you feel depressed sometimes?

High-energy indicators:

a. Do you sleep well and awake refreshed?
b. Are your eyes bright?
c. Do you find pleasure in doing your normal activities?
d. Do you look forward to each day?
e. Do you enjoy being quiet?
f. Do you move gracefully?

This book aims to help you understand your body as the "outer manifestation" of your spirit. Understanding implies both knowing and feeling. In the following chapters, we'll examine the factors that contribute to your energy state and also look at some exercises that will help you feel the difference when you move your body in a more alive, more graceful way.

3
Breathing

THE right to be a person starts with our first breath. How strongly we feel that right is reflected in how well we breathe. If we all breathed as naturally as animals do, our energy level would be high, and we would rarely suffer from chronic tiredness or depression. But most people in our culture breathe shallowly and have a tendency to hold their breath. What is worse, they are not even aware they have a breathing problem. Instead, they race headlong through their lives, stopping occasionally to tell each other that they "barely have time to breathe."

Today, most exercise programs stress the need to breathe deeply, and yoga has long used breathing exercises as part of its physical and spiritual training. But breathing exercises, valuable as they are, do not explain why people find it so difficult to breathe naturally. We shall address that problem in this chapter. But first we need to understand the dynamics of breathing.

As we all know, breathing provides the oxygen necessary to stoke the metabolic fires. Unfortunately, the body does not store oxygen in any significant amount, so that if breathing stops for more than several minutes, death occurs. (In contrast, it is possible to survive without water for a number of days and without food for a number of months.) But breathing is not simply a mechanical operation. It is an aspect of the underlying bodily rhythm of expansion and contraction that also finds expression in the beating of the heart. More than that, it is an expression of the body's spirituality. The Bible states that when God created man he took a piece of clay and breathed life into it. The idea that the air contains some force essential to life is also an important element in Hindu philosophy, in which it is called *prana*. Oxygen is such a vital force that it has the power to cause an inert substance like wood to burst into flame. It has that same property in the living organism.

Breathing is directly connected to the body's state of excitation. When we are relaxed and quiet, our breathing is slow and easy. In a state of high emotion, breathing becomes more rapid and intense. When we are afraid, we breathe in sharply and hold our breath. When we are tense, our breathing becomes shallow. The reverse is also true. Deeper breathing serves to relax the body.

My first experience with the relationship between tension and breathing occurred when I was an ROTC candidate in college. I was practicing shooting on a rifle range, but try as I might, my shots kept missing the bull's-eye. An instructor who was watching me suggested I take three deep breaths and squeeze the trigger slowly while exhaling on the third breath. As long as I held my breath while firing, he said, my body would be tense and my hand would shake. He was right, as I demonstrated with my next shot. This experience impressed me, but I did nothing with it until my therapy with Wilhelm Reich. That therapy made me aware that I often held my breath, a tendency I could counteract by focusing on my breathing. The value of this focus has been demonstrated to me many times while undergoing dental treatment. As I lie in the chair, I focus on breathing easily and deeply while relaxing as much as I can. Unless the dentist is drilling in a very sensitive area, the pain is easily supportable, and I require no novocaine. In the succeeding years after my therapy with Reich, I worked on my breathing, first by becoming more aware of it and then by performing the bioenergetic breathing exercises described later in the chapter. These exercises differ from ordinary breathing exercises in that they encourage a more natural, involuntary kind of deep breathing. I cannot emphasize enough the value of this work for me. It has promoted my health, strengthened my life, and allowed me to function more freely and easily in all situations of stress. It has proved particularly invaluable in public speaking, where it has enabled me to avoid the tension of addressing a large audience.

It is important to be aware of our breathing, to notice whether we breathe through the nose or the mouth, or hold our breath. Sighing is a valuable clue, since it is a response to unconsciously holding the breath. Normal breathing is an audible phenomenon that becomes even more audible when we are asleep. The person who breathes almost inaudibly is severely inhibiting his breathing.

Unlike sighing, which involves letting out air, yawning involves taking in air. A sign of being tired or sleepy, it occurs when our energy needs replenishing. It is also a sign of boredom. When a situation is stimulating and exciting, our breathing is strong, and our energy rises.

Natural breathing—that is, the way a child or an animal

breathes—involves the whole body. Not every part is actively engaged, but every part is affected to a greater or lesser degree by the respiratory waves that traverse the body. When we breathe in, the wave starts deep in the abdominal cavity and flows upward to the head. When we breathe out, the wave moves from head to feet. These waves can easily be observed, as can any disturbance in the breathing process. A common disturbance is an arrest of the wave at the level of the navel or pelvic bones. This prevents the wave from involving the pelvis or deep abdominal cavity in the breathing process and results in shallow breathing. Deep breathing involves the lower abdominal cavity, which balloons out in inspiration and collapses in expiration. This idea may seem confusing, since air never actually enters the abdominal cavity; however, when one breathes deeply, the expansion of the deep abdominal cavity allows the lungs to expand downward more easily and completely. Since this direction allows for the greatest expansion of the lungs, such breathing is both easier and fuller. All young children breathe in this fashion.

In shallow breathing the respiratory movements are limited to the thorax and the diaphragmatic area. The downward movement of the diaphragm is reduced, forcing the lungs to expand outward. This places a strain on the body, since expanding the rigid thoracic cage requires more effort than expanding the abdominal cavity. It is fair to wonder why this is the more common form of breathing, since it requires more work and takes in less oxygen for the effort. The answer to this question lies in understanding the connection between breathing and feeling.

To breathe deeply is to feel deeply. If we breathe deeply into the abdominal cavity, that area becomes alive. By not breathing deeply, we suppress certain feelings associated with the abdomen. One of these feelings is sadness, since the abdomen is involved in deep crying. We speak of such crying as a "belly cry." Belly crying has a depth of sadness that in many cases touches despair. Children learn early in life that by pulling in the belly and making it tight they can cut off painful feelings of sadness and hurt.

It may seem smart and fashionable to have a flat belly. To emphasize their youthfulness, female models in magazines are generally shown with flat, sucked-in bellies. But flatness also denotes an absence of the fullness of life. When we describe something as flat, we mean that it lacks color, excitement, and taste. I have often heard people with flat bellies complain of inner emptiness. A lack of feeling in this part of the body also means that the lovely sexual feelings of warmth and melting in the pelvis are missing. In such an individual sexual excitement is mainly confined to the genital organs. The problem stems from the suppression of sexual feelings in childhood. If one puts some pressure on the belly with a fist, one senses a lack of resistance, as if there is a hole in the lower abdomen. One does not feel this hole when the belly is full and round. It is necessary in such cases to get the person to breathe deep into the belly to restore some life and feeling to the area. Even when an individual becomes conscious that he is not breathing deeply, special exercises are required to activate such breathing. One way is to have the person breathe against the pressure of a hand on the abdomen. In the treatment of emphysema, a serious breathing disorder, patients are often told to breathe against a weight on the belly, lifting it with inhalation and letting it fall slowly upon exhalation. Another way to open up the breathing is to lie on the floor with a rolled-up blanket under the small of the back, with the knees bent and the backside pressing against the floor.[1] Whatever method one uses to get the breath to extend deep enough into the pelvis that one feels it in the pelvic floor, the effect will be to activate suppressed feelings of sadness and sexuality. If we can accept these feelings—and especially if we can cry deeply—the whole body will become radiantly alive. I have seen this happen to many patients.

The significance of the fullness or emptiness of the belly was clearly demonstrated to me by the following incident. A collie that my wife and I had some years ago gave birth to fourteen pups. The last four were stillbirths because their birth was delayed too long, but still, ten pups were more than the dog could nurse at one time. We soon realized that the stronger ones were getting all the milk and that the weaker ones would die. We called a vet for help. His suggestion was to allow the weaker ones to feed first, for when they were finished, the stronger ones would still be able to suck enough milk for their needs. But how could we tell which were the stronger or weaker? We picked up each pup and felt its belly. The ones with bellies that felt full to the touch went into one box; those whose bellies felt empty, into another. The latter got first crack at the nipples. Following this procedure, all ten pups survived to become healthy dogs.

In another kind of breathing disturbance, the chest is rigid and relatively immobile, while breathing is largely diaphragmatic, with some extension into the abdomen. In this condition the chest is overinflated, sometimes to the extent that the person is barrel chested. While the barrel-chested look may seem very manly, it predisposes the person to emphysema. The continued overinflation of the chest so stretches and tears the very fine lung tissue that oxygen uptake by the blood is inadequate despite labored and painful efforts to force more air into the lungs. Even when the inflation is less extreme, it poses a serious threat to health because the rigidity of the chest places an enormous stress on the heart.[2]

The most important breathing experience I ever had occurred during my first session with Wilhelm Reich. Reich had observed in his psychoanalytic practice that when a patient held back the expression of some thought or feeling he would hold his breath. It was a form of resistance, but instead of pointing out the patient's resistance to him, Reich directed him to breathe freely. As soon as the patient opened up his breathing, his thoughts and feelings would pour out. After seeing this time and again, Reich began to focus on breathing as the key to a patient's conscious and unconscious resistance.

During my first session with Reich, I lay on a bed wearing just a pair of shorts so that he could observe my breathing. Reich's only instruction was to breathe. It seemed to me that I was, but after ten minutes Reich said, "Lowen, you're not breathing." I answered that I was breathing; otherwise, I would be dead. He responded, "But your chest isn't moving." Then he asked me to put my hand on his chest to feel how it moved in and out with his inspiration. I saw that my chest wasn't moving as much as his and decided to mobilize mine so that it would move with my breathing. I did that for a number of minutes, breathing through my mouth. Then Reich asked me to open my eyes wide. As I did, a scream broke out of me. I heard the scream but felt detached from it. I didn't feel frightened—just surprised. Reich asked me to stop screaming because it would disturb the neighbors, and I did. I resumed breathing through my mouth, and after about ten minutes Reich again asked me to open my eyes wide. Once again the scream issued out of me, and again I heard it with a sense of detachment. When I left his office, I realized that I had some deep problem of which I was completely unaware. I also realized that deep and free breathing had the power to reach and release suppressed feelings.[3]

Reich devoted succeeding therapy sessions to deep breath-

ing after first asking me to tell him whatever negative thoughts
or feelings about him I had on my mind. This was intended
to bring the negative transference out into the open so that it
could be seen, analyzed, and dispelled. After that initial discussion I would lay on the bed and breathe. If any thoughts
seemed important, I would share them with Reich. However,
the more important thing was to give in to the process of
natural breathing. When I would make an effort to breathe
deeply, Reich would say, "Don't do it, let it happen." At first
I found this confusing, for I was trying to follow his instruc-
tions to the best of my ability. Of course, nothing dramatic
happened. By breathing consciously, I unconsciously controlled the release of feelings. Still, my first session had convinced me of the soundness of Reich's approach, and so I
stayed willingly with the therapy and tried to let my breathing
take its natural course.

In the first month of therapy I regularly experienced paraes-
thesia, or the symptoms of hyperventilation. My hands and
arms would tingle and on one or two occasions became prickly.
On several occasions my hands turned to ice and developed a
carpal spasm. They became like birds' claws and were impossible to move. Reich assured me that these symptoms would pass
as my breathing quieted down, and they did.

Most people who engage in deep breathing while lying quietly will develop the symptoms of hyperventilation. The physi-
ological explanation is that such breathing blows off too much
CO_2 from the blood, which causes this reaction. The treatment is simply to breathe into a paper bag so that some of the
CO_2 is reabsorbed. Strangely, as the therapy progressed I
ceased experiencing any symptoms of hyperventilation when I
let my breathing become deeper and freer. I came to understand that the term *hyper* is relative to the previous depth of
one's breathing; that is, if one breathes more deeply than one

is accustomed to, the symptoms of hyperventilation will develop. When the body has become accustomed to drawing deeper breaths, such "ventilation" is no longer experienced as "hyper."

Another explanation for the same symptoms is that breathing charges the body energetically. If a person's body is unaccustomed to a particular degree of charge or excitation, it will become overcharged, a frightening and painful state. If the increased charge is not released, the body will contract, producing the symptoms described above. But once a person can tolerate a higher charge, the body will feel more alive, which is what happened to me as I relaxed into therapy with Reich. It is also possible to prevent or reduce the symptoms of hyperventilation by kicking a bed or otherwise exerting oneself strenuously enough to discharge the excess energy.

In my own therapy, two other dramatic events happened as I continued to breathe and give in to my body. One time, as I was lying on the bed breathing, something moved me, rocking my body until I sat up on the bed. Without any conscious thought or effort, I got up and stood for a moment facing the bed. Then I began to hit it with both fists. As I did so, I saw the face of my father. I knew that I was hitting him because he had spanked me—an event I had completely forgotten. When I saw my father sometime later, I asked him whether he had ever spanked me. He admitted he had on one occasion when I had worried my mother by returning home late from play.

The experience of rising spontaneously from the bed amazed me. Unlike my first session with Reich, when I had screamed without feeling any fear, this time I felt the full force of my anger. It is important to realize that none of my actions were performed consciously. Something on a deeper level—the level of the id, as Freud called it—propelled me into action.

The concept of acting without the participation of the conscious mind is central to Zen practice and philosophy. In an account of his Zen training to become a master archer, Eugene Harrigel writes that "one reaches the place where one doesn't shoot the arrow. It looses the shot."[4] What is this that acts within us or through us but is not recognized as the self? It is a force, but one that seems to have a mind of its own and an awareness that is deeper and broader than our consciousness. If we need a name, it can only be called the spirit within us that moves us to act.

In other words, experiencing the body's spirituality does not depend on performing but on feeling a force within the self that is greater than the conscious self.

The other turning point in my therapy occurred sometime later. One session, as I lay on the bed breathing, I had the distinct impression that I was on the verge of seeing an image on the ceiling. Over several sessions that premonition became stronger. Then the image appeared. I saw my mother's face looking down at me with a very angry expression. I experienced myself at about nine months of age, lying in a carriage outside the house. I had been crying for my mother, but my crying must have disturbed her, perhaps because she was busy at some task. When she came out, she had such a cold, hard expression on her face that I froze. I realized that the scream I had not uttered then was the scream that emerged in my first session with Reich. It was still caught in my throat, which was so contracted that I could neither scream nor sob. Many years later I had an experience in a workshop I led that added to my understanding. One of the participants suggested that they work with my body to relieve some of my tensions. I agreed. I lay on the floor, and two women worked on me at the same time, one on my tight throat and one on my feet, two areas where the tension was severe. I remember feeling helpless, and

I experienced, at that moment, a sharp pain across my throat, as if it had been cut. I knew that my mother had cut my throat psychologically and that it was difficult for me to speak out or cry out.

The reader will recall that the scream erupted when I mobilized my chest in breathing. The scream was locked in my throat, but the pain of my mother's hostility was locked in my chest. It was the pain of heartbreak at the loss of my mother's love that I had to suppress in order to survive, because when I fought against being weaned by screaming and crying, she turned against me. By immobilizing my chest, I could suppress the pain, but the effect was to impose an enormous stress on my heart. I had lived with an unconscious fear of abandonment that I could release only by facing the fear and crying about my loss.

It is not generally recognized that suppression of a feeling makes one afraid of that feeling. It becomes a skeleton in the closet one dares not look at. The longer it is hidden, the more frightening it becomes. One finds in therapy that when the closet door is opened, that is, when the feeling is evoked, it is never as frightening as one anticipated. One reason is that we are no longer helpless children. Most of us have developed the ego strength to deal with feelings that a child lacks. But that ego strength is not available to deal with suppressed feelings since these are unconscious. Suppressed feelings are like shadows in the night that are magnified by our imagination into nightmarish figures.

If you are a person who tends to hold in feelings, if you have difficulty crying, you are most likely to have some disturbance of your breathing. If you hold in feelings, you will hold in the air, and your chest will probably be overinflated. Women are freer than men in the expression of feeling—they can cry more easily—and consequently their breathing is freer, they suffer fewer heart attacks, and they live longer. This is not to say that they don't have emotional problems or that their breathing is fully natural. Women who pattern themselves on such male values as being tough, efficient, and in control of their feelings are as vulnerable as men and may also have inflated chests. Smokers of either sex are particularly likely to suffer from this condition. Smoking gives the sensation of breathing without introducing much oxygen into the body, oxygen that might stir up painful feelings.

In the interest of health it is important to become aware of our breathing patterns. The following exercise may be of some help in making you aware of your breathing and in deepening it. First note the size of your chest and whether you breathe in strongly. Do you hold in the air for long? If so, you may have as much of a problem letting out your feelings as you do in letting the air out fully.

EXERCISE 3.1

In a sitting position, preferably on a hard chair, make a continuous "ah" sound in your normal voice while looking at the second hand of a watch. If you cannot maintain the sound for at least twenty seconds, you have some respiratory difficulty.

To improve your breathing, repeat this exercise regularly, trying to extend the time you sustain the sound. Although the exercise isn't dangerous, you may feel out of breath. Your body will react by breathing intensely to replenish the oxygen in your blood. Such intense breathing mobilizes the tight chest muscles, allowing them to relax. In the process you may end up crying.

You can also perform the above exercise by counting aloud

in a steady rhythm. The continued use of your voice requires a sustained expiration. This exercise will have the same effect as the preceding one. By breathing out more fully, you will breathe in more deeply.

In this and other exercises, it is important not to force a result. Like all natural functions, breathing naturally simply happens. As you let go and give in to the mysterious power of your body, you will recover your gracefulness and your health.

What about people whose chests are relatively mobile and deflated? This condition is normal if breathing also extends deep into the abdomen. In that case, the respiratory wave traverses the whole body. Often, however, the deflated chest is flat and narrow, with breathing limited to the thorax. Individuals with such a physique have more difficulty breathing in than breathing out. They do not hold in their feelings but cut them off. This is particularly true of the deep-belly feelings of sadness, despair, and desire. The trauma to these individuals in early life was more severe than what most people experience. Their desire for contact was not simply frustrated occasionally but crushed, which made them feel that they had no right to joy or fulfillment; hence, their deep despair.

Most often, a child's desire for loving contact takes the form of a wish to suck on his mother's breast. If the experience of my patients is any indication, this desire is often frustrated. Very few adults know how to suck effectively. An adult who places a thumb in his mouth is likely to suck weakly with his lips. A newborn baby or animal, on the other hand, is likely to suck ferociously with his entire mouth. By pressing the nipple against the hard palate with the tongue while the throat opens to create a vacuum, the newborn is able to draw the maximum amount of milk from the breast. Bottle-fed babies, however, suck largely with the lips; gravity does much of the work for them. Thus, sucking milk from a breast is a more active and aggressive action.

Pediatrician Margaret Ribble clearly showed the intimate connection between sucking and breathing in her book *The Rights of Infants.* [5] Ribble found that when an infant is weaned prematurely—that is, within the first year of life—its breathing becomes shallow and irregular. The infant experiences the loss of the breast as the loss of his world. His distress, in many cases, is enormous, but crying rarely helps. Because the child cannot reestablish his loving connection with the breast, he must suppress his desire in an attempt to avoid the pain of longing. Generally, babies do this by tensing their throat muscles, a habit that carries over into adulthood, where it affects the breathing.

To breathe aggressively, a person needs to feel the action of his throat in the process, just as a baby needs to feel the action of his throat to suck aggressively. One way to mobilize the throat muscles is to groan while inhaling. One can also combine a groan on exhalation with one on inhalation, as the following exercise shows.

EXERCISE 3.2

Use the same sitting position as the previous exercise. Breathe normally for one minute to become relaxed. Now, as you breathe out, make a groaning sound for the length of a complete exhalation. On the inhalation try to make the same sound. It may be difficult at first, but it can be accomplished with a little practice. Do you sense the air being sucked into your body? Just before a sneeze the body sucks in air with such

force that it feels like a vacuum cleaner. Have you experienced
that action?

I have also used this exercise to help people cry when they
find it very difficult to do so. After making the groaning sound
for three full breaths, I ask them to break up the groan of
exhalation into the "ugh, ugh" sounds of sobbing while continuing to vocalize the inhalation. If the exhalation is deep enough
to reach the belly, it will often end in some involuntary crying.

Sometimes when a person begins to cry, he will say in a
surprised tone, "But I don't feel sad." His detachment in the
face of his deepest feelings is similar to my experience of
screaming without sensing my fear.

I generally say to him, "You are sad because you are rigid
or tight." What I mean is that he has lost the feeling of grace.
And since this is true of all of us, we all have something to cry
about.

Nothing helps breathing as much as a good cry. *Crying is our
primary mechanism for releasing tension,* and the only one
available to an infant. We cry not only when we are desperate
but also when our desperation lifts. A mother who has lost a
child doesn't cry while she is frantically searching for him but
only after she has found him. People sometimes cry after orgasm because they, too, have found the lost child within, the
child who once knew the feeling of joy.

While crying is essential to the inflated chest and helpful to
the deflated one, it is not a strong enough action to overcome
that problem. We need a more powerful emotion to mobilize
the aggression necessary to expand the chest fully. That emotion is anger. The individual whose longing has been crushed
has every reason to be angry but lacks the energy to raise and

sustain that feeling to a level of intensity at which it would
become an effective force. The exercise I use for this purpose
is hitting the bed from a standing position. In this exercise the
knees must be bent to provide a flexible support for the action.
The individual raises two fists over his head, keeping the arms
close to the ears and reaching back as far as possible. The
elbows should be slightly bent so that the shoulders are
stretched. The key to this exercise is breathing. From this
position the arms are stretched back slowly three times while
the person breathes in as strongly as possible, filling out the
chest. Following the third strong inspiration, the blow is deliv-
ered, and the air is expelled. In most cases, when this exercise
is done for ten to twenty blows, anger erupts, and the hitting
becomes involuntary. The exercise may also end in spontaneous sobbing when the anger is discharged. The effect is amaz-
ing in many cases. The body becomes charged and alive. One
patient who suffered from feelings of despair and weakness
remarked after the exercise in which he experienced a strong
anger, "I never thought life could be beautiful."

People are more aware of the importance of breathing today
than they were in past years. This is largely due to a heightened
concern about health and to the current knowledge about the
value of exercise and breathing. But we have been brainwashed
by our culture into thinking that there are techniques to
breathing. And so we wish to learn how to *do* it correctly.
Considerable confusion exists about the value of nasal breathing as opposed to mouth breathing.

Many people believe that breathing should be done through
the nose and that the mouth should be kept closed. They
justify this view on the ground that the nose warms and filters
the air, which is supposed to be healthier for the lungs. Mothers often demand that children keep their mouths closed except when speaking or eating. They will add critically, "What

are you trying to do—catch flies? You look stupid with your mouth open." It is true that a dropped jaw gives the face an unfocused look, the opposite of the English expression "Look smart." But why does one have to keep one's wits about one all the time? Why is it necessary always to be in control? As we shall see in a later chapter, a tense jaw plays a key role in the need for control.

Nasal breathing mobilizes the air passages in the head, heightening the senses, especially the sense of smell. Alertness is also increased. Consequently, a person's face looks more alive when he is breathing through his nose. In sleep, a state of diminished alertness, the jaw frequently drops, and breathing is largely through the mouth. Generally, nasal breathing is reserved for quiet and relatively inactive periods. When a person is engaged in strenuous physical activity, he usually breathes through the mouth because of his increased need for oxygen. The same thing is true in strong emotional states like anger, fear, sadness, or passion. In such situations, keeping the mouth closed and breathing through the nose is a way of maintaining control. But there is a time and place for control and for letting go. How one breathes should depend on the situation, not on how a person feels he ought to behave. The body knows how to react appropriately and can be trusted to do so if a person will only let it.

When I give a lecture, I find that it is important to speak slowly and take time out to breathe. Doing so allows me to relax and keep my concentration. But too often I find that my audience is not breathing deeply. Despite their interest, their concentration may flag. When I see them drooping, I stop the presentation and ask them to stretch and take a few good breaths. It makes the lecture so much easier for them to take and me to give. Readers may find themselves in a similar situation, so intent on what they are reading that they uncon-

sciously limit their breathing. For this reason, I want to illustrate the most important breathing exercise in bioenergetics:

EXERCISE 3.3

If you are sitting in a chair reading this book, pause to
breathe. Lean back, raise your arms, and breathe deeply several
times.

Did this stretch enable you to breathe more deeply? When
we sit collapsed, our abdomens are contracted, and deep
breathing is impossible. To straighten out a collapsed abdomen, I use the bioenergetic stool (fig. 3.1). Patients lie over the
stool with their feet on the ground and reach back with their
arms to a chair. This position stretches the muscles of the back,
which must be relaxed if full and easy breathing is to occur. If
one tries not to stiffen against any pain or discomfort, breathing becomes spontaneously deeper and fuller.[6] The first stool
I ever used for this purpose was an old wooden kitchen step
stool on which I placed a rolled-up blanket. If a similar stool
is available to the reader, it can also be used for this purpose.
This arrangement can be used to perform the voice exercises
described earlier. Remember to stop an exercise if it becomes
too painful. Although I know of no one who has been injured
by using the stool or a rolled-up blanket to perform these
breathing exercises, nothing is gained by pushing or forcing.
Natural breathing is a gift of God, who breathed life into our
bodies.

This is an opportune moment to return to the notion that
breathing in, after all, is synonymous with inspiration. Accord-

Figure 3.1. Lying back on the bioenergetic stool.

ing to the dictionary, to inspire is to infuse someone with an animating, quickening, or exalting influence, which is just what the inhalation of oxygen does. We can sometimes breathe life into a person with mouth-to-mouth resuscitation, just as God is reputed to have done with the first man. I can also picture God, after creating the world, stopping to take a good breath, like any honest laborer. As he did so, I have no doubt that he saw it was meaningful and right. As we breathe deeply, it is easy to feel how right the world is, how fair, how beautiful. We are inspired. How tragic it is, then, that so few people breathe freely and well.

4

The Graceful Body: The Loss of Gracefulness

GRACE is a natural attribute of all creatures who live in a state of innocence. Man's fall from grace occurred when he gained knowledge—of good and evil, of right and wrong. No longer was he free to follow his instincts or trust his feelings, certain that they would not betray him. Convinced by the serpent that he would become like a god, he found instead that he was condemned to labor, to earn his bread by the sweat of his brow. Once he ate the fruit of the tree of knowledge, man became self-conscious.

Self-consciousness is both the glory and the curse of humankind. It is the trait that drives man to create and the trait that brings out his inhumanity, cruelty, and greed. Man may see himself as godlike in the magnificence of his achievements, but in his obsession to achieve he is more a madman than a god.

In his self-consciousness he has become a stranger in the natural world. Perhaps *misfit* would be a better word, for it reflects modern man's growing awareness that he is not fit. Some people take their lack of fitness literally and try to run marathons or to pump iron. But these do not make them fit to live as part of the natural order of life, to feel their connection to the universe, or even to know the joy of being alive and healthy. For that they must anchor their self-consciousness in a consciousness of self.

These two concepts are different, though they sound alike. To be self-conscious, a person must stand outside of himself, much as I did when I heard myself scream without experiencing any fear. Self-consciousness denotes a split in the personality, which may range from a crack to a full break as in schizophrenia. This concept is discussed more fully in chapter 8. To be conscious of the self, on the other hand, a person must perceive the feeling state of the body.

We are all familiar with the story about the centipede who, when he tried to think which leg to move first, couldn't move at all. Fortunately for the centipede and for us, all the important functions of the body are self-regulatory. However, in contrast to the centipede, we humans are able to think about certain actions and movements and consciously program them into our behavior. But when we do, we risk treating the body as a machine and destroying its gracefulness. The ego in its relation to the body is like a rider on a horse. If he imposes his will, he can make the animal do whatever he wants, but he will have sacrificed the horse's natural grace. If he guides the horse, allowing it to respond with its feelings, horse and rider will become one in movements that are graceful and pleasurable. This analogy is important because as humans we have two modes of action: voluntary and involuntary. Voluntary movements—walking, writing a book, preparing a meal—are under the control of the ego and subject to the conscious will. Some involuntary movements—blinking, twitching, breathing— occur whether we want them to or not. Others, however, can be stopped by the mind but are considered involuntary because they are spontaneous. We make many gestures in the course of a conversation that are not willed actions; that is, they are not preconceived movements. Similar spontaneous movements occur all the time; we put a hand to our mouth or face, clasp our hands together, move a leg when sitting. Often we are not aware of the movement unless we focus our attention on it. Voluntary movements, in contrast, have a conscious purpose. We brush our teeth, put on our clothes, and eat our food with conscious intent.

The range of voluntary actions is small compared to that of the involuntary movements constantly occurring in the body. Even if we leave aside the movements of the internal organs, we all experience countless small movements on the surface of the body. The body is literally in constant motion, even when we are asleep.

The involuntary movements are a direct manifestation of the aliveness of the body. An artist friend who was painting a portrait remarked about his subject, "Her face is so alive I can't capture the expression." Voluntary or controlled movements do not give that impression. They have a mechanical quality. However, most of the larger movements of the body are not one or the other but a combination of both. The less one's will enters into a movement, the more spontaneous and graceful it is. If our actions are to be graceful and effortless, the ego must trust the unconscious enough to respond to its direction freely and fully.

A lack of gracefulness is a sign of dis-ease. Because such dis-ease is inescapable in our culture, it is rare to find graceful bodies in the adult population. Watching people in the street, one cannot help but be impressed by how awkwardly most of them move. What is even sadder is how unaware they are of their lack of gracefulness. Many are also unaware that they have major emotional problems. Although studies have shown that mental illness is widespread in our culture, most people do not regard their personal symptoms of depression, anxiety, and insecurity as serious emotional problems, which they are. And few see the connection between these so-called mental disturbances and the lack of gracefulness. The confusion arises because medicine does not operate with an understanding of health, but only with some knowledge of illness, which is always seen as a disturbing symptom or malfunction. Most therapies, analytic and otherwise, suffer from this limited view that focuses on the presenting symptom and not on the individual's general health or dis-ease. Since every personality disturbance affects both the body and the mind equally, we must see the psychological problem as a reflection of the physical one and vice versa. Effective therapy that aims at promoting health must be based on an understanding of how and why the individual fell from grace.

Some years ago I treated a successful attorney who consulted me because he was having problems with his girlfriend. He complained that she was afraid of committing herself to the relationship, although they had been sexually intimate. My patient, whom I will call Paul, claimed that he loved his girlfriend deeply and could not understand why she was reluctant to marry him, since she had declared her love for him on several occasions.

Paul was an attractive man in his late forties who had been married, raised three sons, and was now divorced. The reason he gave for the divorce was that his wife had been too dependent on him, which drained the excitement out of the marriage. He led an active life, was engaged in two major sports, and seemed to have a lot to offer a woman. Usually easygoing and relaxed, he was never pushy except in relation to this woman.

Undoubtedly, both people in a relationship contribute to the problem between them. But knowing only Paul, I had to understand the problem in terms of his personality. He spoke easily and was open about his feelings. In this situation, my only clue to his problem lay in observing how his body looked and moved. His body was well built, strong, and compact, but when I asked Paul to lie down on the bioenergetic stool to see how freely he breathed, I was surprised to see that his back was as stiff as a board and his breathing quite limited. Perhaps, I thought, his relaxed, easygoing manner was something he had adopted to impress others and to compensate for his state of inner tension. Or perhaps under his laid-back style was a very controlling ego. Paul admitted that he generally got what he wanted in life, and so his inability to snare this woman upset him greatly despite his very high degree of self-control. I could only guess that Paul's need to control himself and others was an enormous factor in his friend's reluctance to commit herself to him. He could accept neither her need for independence nor her reluctance to be involved. Despite a most pleasing manner, he was not a gracious person.

Paul found it difficult to accept my interpretation of his problem. He could not, however, deny the rigidity of his back, so he accepted the need to work with his body. He bought a stool and used it fairly regularly at home to loosen and relax his back muscles. As he let go somewhat on the physical level, he was also able to let go of his girlfriend. If she had yielded to him, their relationship might well have ended the way his marriage had, in the loss of his interest.

In many ways Paul's relationship with his women friends paralleled that with his mother. His mother was a dependent person who tied her son to her in the name of love. On the surface Paul was a very independent person, but his spirit wasn't free. He was tied to the need to prove himself—to be successful, to achieve, to accept challenges and win. He was always active. The simple pleasure of being was unknown to him.

Paul was a self-conscious individual, living by ego values instead of bodily ones. Ego values are related to the satisfaction one gets from achieving a goal. A bodily value is the physical pleasure one experiences in any activity that is gracefully done. If one focuses on reaching a goal, one sacrifices the pleasure of moving toward it. For example, skiing is an activity that people might well undertake for the immediate excitement and pleasure of gliding effortlessly down a mountain. But too many skiers are intent only upon their performance. They are constantly judging themselves as to how well they did. And even though nothing is achieved in skiing, they have a goal: to ski better today than the day before. Of course, to reach the point where skiing is effortless, one does have to pay attention to how one skis, for skiing is not a natural activity. But the modern skier is constantly looking for an expert trail or a more difficult hill. In that striving he is focused not on pleasure but on accomplishment. Paul was such a skier.

By developing one's skill in any activity, one does become more graceful, at least to all outward appearances. An expert skier looks quite graceful gliding down a mountain. A ballet dancer looks elegant performing the choreographed steps of a show. However, too often there is no correlation between the gracefulness of a learned skill and the natural gracefulness of the body. Watching ballet dancers walk down a street, I have been struck time and again by how awkwardly they walk. The fifth position, the ballet stance where the feet are turned out, may allow them to perform with grace, but by tensing the muscles of the hips and buttocks, it makes it difficult for them to take a graceful step offstage.

If training is not to destroy the natural gracefulness of the body, it must not run counter to the body's flow of excitation. When that flow is strong, one can direct it to produce a graceful and effective action, but if the flow is broken, the spirit of the organism is broken along with it. Then, no matter how effective a learned action is, it will look and feel mechanical. A horse trainer knows that a horse whose spirit has been broken will never be a real winner. Parents, unfortunately, are not always so knowledgeable. One woman with whom I was working spoke about the difficulty she was having controlling her son. She said, "I'll break him," with such vehemence that I realized how much hostility she harbored toward him. I told her I could not work with her, since I could not accept such an attitude on the part of a person who was coming to me for help. No doubt she had been broken when she was a girl, but that in no way justified her attitude toward her child.

Grace and health depend on striking a balance between the ego and the body, between the will and the wish. Chinese philosophy describes the two primary forces in any organism as yin and yang, or sky energy and earth energy. In effect, yang represents a force acting from above; yin, a force acting from below. Too much or too little of one or the other disturbs the balance on which health depends. The relationship between ego and body, will and wish, can also be likened to the relationship between a horse and a rider. Like a horse cantering along, a wish provides the motive power for an action. Meanwhile, the will provides direction and control, just as a rider would. But it is not the function of the will to curb the spirit.

Unfortunately, in our culture the will determines much of our activity in opposition to the body's desire. We have to get up and go to work whether our bodies are rested or tired and whether we are excited or bored by the day's activities. Certainly it is necessary to earn a living, and the will's prodding to get us out of bed may be lifesaving in this regard. But the need to earn a livelihood, to obtain food, clothing, and shelter, is also a bodily desire. Can we say the same for the seemingly imperative drive of some people to become rich, powerful, and famous? The body has no such desires.

Drive is the key word here. Whenever we are driven, we lose our gracefulness, and the body becomes a machine. Here it is appropriate to quote the biblical injunction What value is there in gaining the world if one loses his soul? Man is the only creature who drives himself to the point where he loses his connection to God, life, and nature.

In my view, a major factor in the drive for success and power is an underlying wish to be loved. But while success may produce acclaim, it does not elicit any genuine love. To be loved, one needs to be lovable—that is, able to love. To be lovable, one needs to be humble, to reach out, to open one's heart and be vulnerable. But the willful person is proud. Having been hurt as a child when he was open and vulnerable, he is determined not to suffer that pain and humiliation again. He will command love by his power and position. He will prove his superiority, but he will not cry or ask for love. The intensity of his drive is in direct proportion to his hunger for love, but it serves only to frustrate that desire.

Movements stemming from wishes are spontaneous, in contrast to the deliberate movements ordered by the will. In a healthy person, spontaneous movements are never chaotic or inappropriate unless such movements have been suppressed and are only now breaking through the blocks to their expression. Such breakthroughs are necessary if spontaneity is to become an essential part of a person's behavior, but the proper place for them is in a therapy session where they can be understood in relation to past events.

The human spirit longs to recover its natural grace, to break free from its imprisonment by the ego, to sense its participation in the universal flow. Although the will cannot dictate a return to gracefulness, occasionally an individual will step out of the program imposed by his ego and become freely spontaneous in a natural way. I recall a simple experience that dramatized this phenomenon for me. I was playing baseball, and as I stepped up to the plate to bat, I knew I would hit a home run. My conscious mind did not direct my actions, and I made no special effort to hit the ball well or hard. Yet I swung the bat at the first pitch and hit a home run. It was a mystical experience. I had no control over the swing, and I could explain my home run only by assuming that I was so attuned to the situation that I could not miss. The "it" that hit the ball so perfectly is the same "it" that loosed the arrow of the Zen archer. Almost everyone to whom I have described this event has had a similar experience. I believe such prescience is based on an unconscious awareness of the operative forces in a situation. This attunement is a result of the body's spirituality that is undermined when the logical mind imposes a strict cause and effect relationship on behavior.

I believe that waves of excitation in a body send their vibrations into the surrounding space. Some of these vibrations are in the form of sound waves that carry the voice; others are more subtle. Many people, however, can sense other people's "vibes" all the same. When such empathy occurs at a distance, as when a person becomes aware of the death of a loved one residing in another city, it seems unbelievable. Yet it is hard for me to dismiss the large number of reports from so many different people who have had such experiences.

Thick-skinned people and those who live in a shell rarely experience such "coincidences" because the rigidity of their bodies prevents them from vibrating in resonance with others. But having a thin skin is no guarantee of health. Schizophrenics are known to be hypersensitive to what is happening around them, and many have extrasensory experiences. In their case, the boundary of the self is too porous, which in psychological terms means that the ego is deficient in maintaining an effective barrier against incoming stimuli. Such people are prone to be overwhelmed.[1]

In a healthy organism, there is a balance between containment and excitation; the individual feels free to express his impulses and feelings, yet has the self-possession to know how to do so appropriately and effectively. In such individuals, the mind and body are as intimately connected as the yin and yang in the "circle of the whole." They are conscious of the self, not self-conscious. Every movement involves the whole person in a unified way.

From what has been said above, it is clear that the key to gracefulness is to allow the body to move itself. That process is destroyed early in life because parents mistrust the ability of the body to regulate itself. Even in such a simple matter as eating, precious few children are allowed to follow their own impulses and desires but instead are ordered to eat what parents consider to be a proper and adequate diet. It is true that children, if left alone, may gorge themselves on junk food but, generally, this tendency will pass unless the child has serious emotional difficulties. It is far more harmful for parents to force children to eat what they don't want than to let them eat junk food occasionally. Sometimes parents go to the extreme of sending a child to bed because he would not eat what was set before him. I knew of a case where the child was forced to eat his vomitus to teach him that he had to obey his parents and eat what they had ordered. Even with so many stories of child abuse currently circulating, it is shocking to hear about such cruelty to children by their parents. It runs against our faith and trust in the parent-child relationship.

Today's parents are under great pressure to get so many things done that they are impatient with children. In comparison with a parent a child has all the time in the world: time to play, time to be carefree, time to be joyous. A child is not yet part of the grown-up world of drives and goals, a fact that can drive parents up the wall. Don't dawdle, keep moving, get it done, parents say. But by pressuring a child in this way, they effectively kill much of the pleasure the child may have in his activities and movements. Once "getting it done" becomes the most important thing, gracefulness is lost. If a person is interested in recovering some of his lost grace, he must understand the critical role that time plays. In the modern world, time is money. Only in childhood, and only for some few unhurried children, is it pleasure.

The following exercise is helpful in illustrating how the tyranny of time robs one of gracefulness.

EXERCISE 4.1

Choose any activity that you normally do, such as walking, cleaning your house, preparing a meal, or writing a letter.

Let's start with walking. Are you aware that you are often in such a hurry to get somewhere that you are barely conscious of walking? Do you sense how ungraceful your movements are? Try to slow down so you can feel every step, but don't *think* about how to walk. Instead, let your body walk you at its own pace. The conscious "you" is merely going along for the ride. If this exercise makes you feel awkward, you have become self-conscious about walking. In other words, you are judging your style or thinking about how other people see you. Instead, focus your attention fully on the sensation of walking. See if you can feel the pleasure of being alive, moving freely without care.

In a world as hectic and pressured as ours, it is not easy to maintain a rhythm that differs from the common pace. It used to be that whenever I returned from a winter vacation in the Caribbean I would find as I walked to my office that everyone on the street was passing me by. Unfortunately, by the second week I would find that I was moving as fast as they were. But this is one bad habit I've been able to break. I now make it a practice to walk slowly, and I find that it has greatly increased my pleasure. In fact, I sometimes try to walk as slowly as I can. When I do, the feeling of aliveness in my feet and legs sometimes extends through my whole body.

The same exercise can be applied to any other activity— even, for example, washing dishes, a job I sometimes do, just like any other modern man. My wife complains that although I get the job done quickly the dishes are never spotless, and she often has to go over them again. I realize that I do the dishes quickly because I want to get the job over with. Obviously I don't really enjoy the activity. But it is impossible to enjoy an activity if one is rushing to get it done. When I can control my drivenness and slow down, I find that I do derive some pleasure out of washing dishes. The reason that cleanliness is next to godliness, after all, is that it is a sign of order, a mark of God's work in creating the universe out of chaos.

As the foregoing has illustrated, mindfulness—or an unpressured self-awareness—helps one harness one's natural grace. So does allowing movement to flow through the whole body instead of limiting it to a part. As the following exercise demonstrates, even extending the hand to greet someone can mobilize the body from head to toe—if we will only let it.

EXERCISE 4.2

The exercise involves the simple movement of reaching out a hand to greet someone or to give something. Stand with your feet parallel, about eight inches apart. Bend your knees slightly. This will be your basic standing position, which I will elaborate on in a later chapter.

Reach out your arm as if to give or greet. Return it to your side to try again. This time, before you reach out your arm, press the corresponding foot into the ground and lean forward slightly as you extend your arm. The wave that produces the movement should start from the ground and traverse your whole body.

Did the gesture feel different? Could you sense how your whole body was involved? Do you see a difference between an action that involves the whole body and a movement that lacks this quality?

In this chapter I have examined the question of gracefulness from the perspective of the conflict between the ego and the body. This conflict engenders a split between thinking and feeling, the will and the wish, control and abandon, and the upper and lower halves of the body. When the upper half of the body dominates the personality, we lose our natural gracefulness. To restore the spirituality of the body, we need to reverse this attitude: we need to move from the ground in response to feeling. As we have just seen, a graceful movement starts in the lower part of the body and flows upward and outward following the wave of excitation. In the next chapter we will study the nature of feelings, which result when the wave of excitation reaches the surface of the body.

5
Feeling and Feelings

I HAVE said that the spirituality of the body is the feeling of connectedness to the universe. A feeling is not just an idea or a belief; it is more than a mental process, since it involves the body. It consists of two elements, a bodily activity and a mental perception of that activity. Thus, it can be regarded as the unifying force between mind and body, connecting the conscious mind to bodily activity. The latter by itself does not give rise to a feeling. In sleep, for example, the body may move strongly but there is no feeling, since the conscious mind is dulled (asleep). But one can have a mind that is aware and alert without feelings if there is no spontaneous movement in the body. If a person lets his arm hang absolutely motionless by his side for several minutes, he loses the feeling of his arm. On the other hand, it is possible for the body to be active without giving use to feelings if there is a split between the perceiving organ, the ego, and the object of perception, the body. This disturbance is typical of the narcissistic personality.

As long as a person is alive, he is not completely devoid of feeling even in the narcissistic state. One can feel sensations such as heat, cold, pain, pressure, etc. Missing in this personality or greatly reduced are the feelings we call emotions: namely, fear, anger, sadness, love, etc. These feelings arise from spontaneous movements in the body representing impulses to reach out to, or withdraw from, the environment. The impulse to reach out represents the desire for pleasure and fulfillment. It gives rise to a feeling of love if one is conscious of the impulse. The impulse to withdraw would be the response to the experience or anticipation of pain and would give rise to a feeling of fear. One could also react by striking out to eliminate the threat, which would give rise to a feeling of anger. But it is not necessary for the impulse or reaction to be acted out for a feeling to occur. When an impulse reaches the surface, resulting in a readiness to act, a feeling arises whether the action is carried out or not. One can be angry without attacking, frightened without running, or sad without crying, because there is perception of the impulse. However, some people speak of love without sensing an impulse to reach out for contact in a warm and tender way. In that case, love is a thought, not a feeling.

In the following discussion I will speak of feelings and emotions. To avoid confusion, it must be recognized that every emotion is a feeling but not every feeling is an emotion. Love, anger, and fear are typical emotions that are also called feelings. Sensations like hot and cold, pain or pressure, tastes and smells, are feelings but not emotions. The word *emotion* has an action component (*motion* plus *e* as a prefix means to move out) that distinguishes this kind of feeling from others. Also, emotions are experienced as total body responses. I may, for example, have a feeling of pain in my lower back; but when I am angry, the feeling is not localized or limited—I am angry all over. However, impulses associated with the different emotions vary and have different pathways to expression.

A functional understanding of feeling needs to be based on the energetic processes in the living body. These are of two kinds: (1) a generalized pulsatory activity in the organs and in the body as a whole and (2) specific impulses and reactions, as described above. Movements of expansion and contraction are the manifest signs of the life force in an organism. This rhythmic pulsation is most evident in a jellyfish, a very primitive animal. Anyone who has watched one of these creatures closely cannot help but be impressed by its ability to propel itself through the water by expanding and contracting. As we have seen, the most obvious manifestation of this life force in humans is the in and out of breathing. Similar rhythms also exist in the peristaltic activity of the intestines and the beating of the heart. Actually, all living cells breathe. They take in oxygen and expel carbon dioxide in a process known as internal respiration that is the basic pulsatory activity of life.

Since these movements of expansion and contraction are spontaneous, it is fair to ask whether feeling states are associated with them, at least in people. In my experience, they are. When a patient's breathing becomes free, easy, and deep in the course of bioenergetic therapy, I generally notice a quiet peacefulness well up in him. If I ask him how he feels, the invariable answer is "I feel good." While no specific emotion is connected to this state, it does have a feeling quality. A patient has never responded, "I don't feel anything." Such a statement would indicate a diminution in the normal intensity of the body's pulsatory activity and is far likelier to come from someone who is clinically depressed. Health, therefore, is not the absence of pain but the presence of a basic pleasure tone in the body.

Our ability to sense what is happening to another person, an ability I have described as empathy, is based on the fact that our bodies resonate with other living bodies. If we don't resonate with others, it is because we don't resonate within ourselves. If a person can say, "I don't feel anything," then he has cut off not only the feeling of his own aliveness but any feeling he might have for others, both people and beasts.

To survive, an organism must be sensitive to its environment. That sensitivity resides in the membrane that encloses the organism, a selectively permeable membrane that allows food and essential elements to enter and waste products to leave. Selectivity, or the ability to distinguish between different stimuli, is the basis for awareness and consciousness. Thus, it is accurate to say that consciousness is a surface phenomenon.

Our awareness of the world depends largely on the functioning of our major sense organs, all of which are specialized skin (or surface) structures. The information these organs receive is relayed via the nerves to the brain, where it is projected on the mind's screen so that we can react to incoming stimuli. However, no particular feeling accompanies the information. Feeling depends on the nature of our responses. If our response is positive—that is, if the stimulus evokes an expansive movement in the body—we will experience a feeling of pleasure and excitement. If our response is negative—that is, if the stimulus provokes a contraction in the body—we will experience a feeling of fear or pain. We attribute these feelings to the stimuli themselves, but in reality they are the perceptions of our responses. If we were anaesthetized so that no response was possible, we would feel nothing at all.

Our actions, however, are not determined solely by the stimuli that impinge on our bodies. We also respond to impulses that arise spontaneously from within. These impulses are related to our needs: the need for excitement gives rise to an impulse to reach out for contact with another body, while the need for food gives rise to an impulse to eat. These internal movements also give rise to feelings when they reach the surface of the body and the brain, where perception occurs.

The following figures, 5.1 and 5.2, reduce these processes to their simplest terms. In figure 5.1 the organism is represented by a sphere somewhat like a single cell. The center, corresponding to the nucleus of a cell, represents the energy source of all movements. An impulse, or wave of excitation, moves from the center to the periphery, where expression occurs. At the same time, stimuli impinge on the surface of the cell from without, giving rise to internal reactions.

In higher organisms, the ego has a motor as well as a perceptual function. Because the voluntary muscles of the body are controlled by nerves that have their origin in the conscious centers of the brain, it is the ego that controls all conscious action. This system of voluntary muscles, shown in figure 5.2 as a series of wavy lines, lies close to the surface of the body and constitutes an inner sheath. Every impulse must engage this system as it seeks expression. The ego can, therefore, direct or even block the expression of an impulse by contracting the necessary muscles, thus preventing them from acting. An impulse blocked in this way cannot give rise to a feeling because it cannot reach the surface where perception occurs.

In certain situations, a person may consciously block an impulse from expression. He may have an impulse to strike someone who is causing him pain, for example, but realizing that the aggressor is bigger and stronger, he may decide wisely to restrain that impulse. In such a situation, however, he is well aware of his anger and of the tension created by holding his aggressive impulse in check. If the situation changes or he removes himself from it, he can release the tension and express his anger verbally or by kicking or hitting some object. It is a different story if the situation doesn't change or he cannot

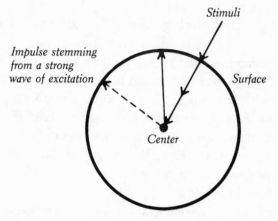

Figure 5.1. Reactions of the organism to stimulation.

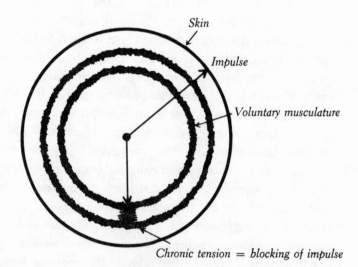

Figure 5.2. The effect of an impulse on the musculature. An impulse activates the musculature but can be blocked by chronic tension and prevented from reaching the surface.

leave. A child may be caught in this bind. He may rightfully feel angry at the hostile behavior of a parent, but chances are he will not be able to express his own anger for fear of retaliation. In our culture, bringing up children often entails a fight or struggle in which the child's freedom is forcibly curtailed and his spirit broken. Parents are free to hit children, but woe to the child who strikes back. After an altercation with a parent, I have often seen an angry child muttering to himself but not daring to speak up. In such a situation, a child has no alternative but to submit, which means that his anger must be suppressed.

When an impulse is consciously held back, the resulting contraction of the muscles is acute. Waves of excitation still reach the muscles, which are all a-quiver like racehorses raring to go but restrained by their jockeys. When the tension becomes chronic, however, the muscles become fixed and the holding back of the impulse becomes unconscious. A fixed, tense muscle makes a spontaneous movement impossible, so that one is no longer aware of anger or any other feeling, not even of the fact that one is holding back feeling. Sensitivity in the area is deadened, so that one doesn't feel the tension. Years later, when the muscle weakens, pain develops, but by this time the individual cannot make a connection between the pain, the tension, and the suppression of feeling. The chronic tension in the musculature that prevents an impulse from activating the muscle and thus being experienced is shown in figure 5.2 as a solid block.

The degree of suppression of a feeling like anger varies in different individuals according to the severity of the threat that occasioned the suppression in the first place. Some individuals find it extremely difficult to feel or express anger; others are able to feel some anger if the provocation is strong enough. Then there are those individuals who fly off the handle at the slightest provocation. One finds that the degree of tension in such people is so severe that it constitutes a constant provocation. Because these explosions of rage occur without the ego's participation—that is, before the person is aware how angry he is and why—they do not serve to release the chronic tension.

Chronically tense muscles give the body a rigid quality and destroy its gracefulness by blocking the flow of excitation. Contracted muscles in any part of the body have a restrictive effect on respiration because full respiration requires the respiratory waves to traverse the whole body. By limiting the fullness and depth of breathing, chronic muscular tension also decreases a person's energy, which diminishes the overall aliveness of the body. As a result, the suppression of one feeling tends to decrease feeling in general. If anger is suppressed, love, sadness, and fear tend also to be reduced, although not necessarily to the same degree. In many people, the body is split so that some feelings are more blocked than others. This explains why some men find it easier to express anger than to cry, while the opposite is true for many women.

Emotions are the direct expression of a person's spirit. One can gauge the strength of an individual's spirit by the intensity of his feelings, the bigness of his spirit by the depth of his feelings, and the ease of his spirit by the quietness of his feelings. When one moves with feeling, the movement is graceful because it is the result of an energetic flow in the body. Thus, feeling is the key to grace and to the spirituality of the body.

Having discussed feelings in general, we can examine the specific emotions of love, anger, fear, sadness, and joy. Love is expansive, strongly charging the surface of the body with energy, resulting in a soft, warm, glowing quality in the body that is a pleasure to see. Love is warm, and the amount of love one feels or expresses is directly proportional to the amount of softness and heat in the body—and so we speak of the heat of passion. The impulse in the emotion of love is to reach out for contact and closeness with the loved person in anticipation of the pleasure that would result.[1]

People who reach out in situations where they can reasonably know they will get hurt are described as masochistic. Masochism seems to contradict the above definition of love, but it can be understood by recognizing that most people suffer from some degree of ambivalence—feelings of love and hate toward the same individual. This ambivalence often stems from a conflicted relationship, for when a child is hurt by a parent, its love for the parent becomes mixed with anger and hate. Throughout life, such a person will retain his love, but the hate and anger will also be there, though it may be suppressed. The suppression, masking the memory of the original childhood conflict, will leave him open to being hurt again as he reaches out for love. Such ambivalence will also be manifested in the way an individual expresses love.

When love turns cold, it changes into hate. We can say that hate is frozen love, which means that the impulse to reach out is suppressed or frozen. The feeling of hate denotes, therefore, a previous feeling of love for the hated object that is buried beneath an outer layer of ice. Love never fully dies, for if it did, the heart, too, would freeze, resulting in death. Thus, it is possible for an individual to proclaim his love even though his behavior and demeanor belie his avowal. Because of the polar relationship between love and hate, it is not uncommon for a feeling of hate to turn into one of love when the impulse to reach out breaks through the shell. Hate is a secondary reaction to the experience or threat of being hurt by someone loved. The first and immediate reaction is sadness and anger. If these feelings are expressed, one doesn't freeze. The suppression of these feelings by chronic muscular tension creates the frozen shell that imprisons the heart and the feeling of love. It also imprisons the spirit, breaking its connection to the universal spirit. Sadness is the natural reaction to the loss of love. Anger, too, is related to love. We don't get angry at people we don't care about; we walk away from them. We become angry with those we love when they hurt us by frustrating our desire to enjoy the closeness of love.

Just as we reach out softly in love, we strike out sharply in anger. But, while in anger we attempt to remove an obstacle to love, in rage we see the object of our anger as an enemy, as one who seeks our destruction. We speak of feeling a "murderous rage," of "wanting to kill" someone. Often such rage is turned on innocent people, especially children. Nothing can so enrage a parent as a rebellious or disobedient child. The parent reacts as if the child, by obstructing his will or denying his power, is inflicting a mortal injury on the parent. Often such rage stems from an injury that had been inflicted upon the parent when he himself was a child—the breaking of his spirit when he was punished severely for daring to stand up to an authoritarian, nonloving parent. The suppression of his anger at this cruel treatment locks it into the parent's personality, where it may smolder for years, until one day it breaks out against someone who is innocent and helpless. The message of this rage is very clear: "Why should you [the child] be a free spirit when I was crushed?" The parent's envy of the child leads to rage.

The concept of a "broken spirit" is not a metaphor or a psychological construct; rather, it is a physical reality in the body of the individual. I believe that every person whose spirit was broken has a suppressed rage that is locked into the muscular tension in upper back and shoulders. This tension can be seen as a break in the natural line of the back, as an exaggerated convexity just below the shoulders, or in the lower back as a lordosis or as a flattening of the natural curve in this area.[2] This flattening of the curve in the lower back forces the pelvis forward, destroying any feeling of cockiness in the person. The position is equivalent to that of a dog with its tail between its legs. Sometimes, pointing this condition out to a patient, I would say, "It is as if your ass were kicked in." One of the traumas that produces this condition is severe or repeated spankings. The excessive curvature of the upper or lower back breaks the straight erect posture that is the hallmark of the free spirit. The chronic tension in the muscles of the back impedes the flow of excitation along the backbone that is experienced as being a free spirit. In effect, one's spirit is broken, and as long as that is so, one will have a murderous rage in him whether he is conscious of it or not. And as long as that rage is unexpressed, he will remain broken. Expressing the rage can have a healing effect once the person understands its origin in the loss of grace.

However, acting out the rage against those who did not break one's spirit—that is, upon individuals who are younger, weaker, or dependent—does not have a positive effect because one cannot feel good about such behavior. It leads to guilt and increases the tension. The proper place to release rage is in a therapy situation where one can let go of control because the therapist is in control. The patient pounds a bed; if he is a man, he uses his fists, if a woman, she uses a tennis racket to feel more potent. By reaching the arms upward and backward one straightens the back and stretches the contracted muscles. The hitting is generally accompanied by such words as "I'll smash you" or "I'll kill you." This technique for releasing rage and other means of diminishing tension, reducing rigidity, and venting suppressed feelings are discussed more fully in chapter 8.

Much as it is important to express one's rage, it is not the main therapeutic objective, which is, as mentioned earlier, the recovery of grace. Expressing rage provides only a temporary release of the tension and does not heal the person's spirit. In smashing an object, we tense our shoulder muscles to gain more power, but in the process we lose our gracefulness. We need to strike out in a different way—not with the idea of smashing or destroying but at the same time to guard our integrity and protect our spirit. We need to learn how to express our anger, which, in contrast to rage, is a graceful action because it is a flowing movement. In hitting the bed with anger, the individual stretches his body upward from his feet, reaching back with his arms as much as possible. The arms are then swung for the blow loosely, easily, and freely. If it is done correctly, the wave of energy or excitation flows throughout the whole body from feet to hands in a graceful action. The appropriate expression of anger frees the spirit.

Reaching out for loving contact is an aggressive movement. The only difference between reaching out with the arms in love or striking out with them in anger is that the former movement is gentle and soft, whereas the latter is forceful and hard. Although the feeling is different in these actions, the strength of the feeling is directly proportional to the length of the stretch. A full extension of the arms expresses a full feeling. If, however, the shoulders are tied up because anger has been suppressed, the extent of the reach is shortened, and the feeling is weakened.

Emotions come in pairs that are polar opposites, such as love and hate, joy and sadness, anger and fear. From an energetic point of view, fear must be understood as the opposite of the impulse of anger. In the face of a threat or danger one could strike out in anger or withdraw in fear. Both emotions move along the same pathways: In anger the movement of the wave of excitation is outward, flowing upward through the muscles of the back, raising the back in preparation for an attack, as a cat or dog does, then moving into the arms or teeth. The flow toward the teeth, our primary organ of attack, passes over the top of the head. I have personally experienced the flow of that wave of excitation going into my canine teeth. In fear, by contrast, the flow of excitation is reversed: Imitating an expression of fear will enable one to sense that direction. The eyeballs roll upward, the head is pulled back, contracting the neck, and the shoulders are raised. The whole body contracts and tightens. If the fear is a momentary sensation, the contraction will release when the danger passes. Sometimes fear produces anger as a rebound wave of excitation. Scare a child and you will see his anger flare.

Fear has a paralyzing effect on the spirit. It freezes the body, contracting the muscles. When this state persists, the body becomes numb, and the individual no longer feels his fear. This is the state in which most people come to therapy. They are depressed but not frightened, not even sad. The therapeutic task is to get the person in touch with his fear by getting him to feel the tensions in his body. As he attempts to mobilize the contracted areas he will sense fear. If he feels the fear, he may be afraid that the therapist will hurt him—a projection, of course, of the fear he felt of his father or mother. But he may also be afraid of the impulses behind the fear, especially the impulse of anger—or more correctly, rage—that could be murderous.

If the physical tension of fear is chronic, its release can be achieved only by turning it into anger, that is, by changing the direction of the energetic movement. The anger can be expressed by hitting, biting, kicking, twisting a towel (good substitute for a neck), and other means. All these actions are used in therapy to release the tension and restore the body's freedom and gracefulness of movement. This technique is fully effective only if the individual is aware of his fear. Without that awareness the procedures described above are only exercises, even if they evoke a strong feeling of anger.

Most of us are also afraid of the sadness that we carry within. If we let ourselves cry, we become frightened because the sadness feels like a bottomless pit or like a deep well in which we would drown if we let go. There is a bottom to our sadness, but just before we reach the bottom, we will experience a feeling of despair that can be terrifying. One can take a patient through his despair by helping him realize that it stems from and is related to the experiences of his childhood. Patients ask, "How much crying do I have to do before I am free of my sadness? It seems I've been crying a long time." My answer is that it is not a matter of crying a long time but of crying deeply enough to reach the bottom of the well, the pit of the belly. When the convulsive wave of the sobbing extends to the pelvic floor, a trap door opens, allowing the person to emerge into the sunshine. That trap door is the genital apparatus through which rebirth occurs with orgasm.

In addition to the emotions we have discussed—love, anger, and fear—there are generalized feeling states that do not qualify as emotions. One such feeling state is humiliation, which, like the emotions, can be suppressed so that the individual is unaware of it. Nonetheless, this state will often be expressed in the body as a bowing and lowering of the head. The opposite state, which is the feeling of pride, is expressed in a head held high.

A single incident of humiliation will not cause an attitude to become structured in the body. Many women, however, were subjected as children to constant humiliation for any overt expression of sexuality. Sexual abuse in any form is a very humiliating experience for a child, and I would regard spanking as a form of sexual abuse, since the attack is directed at an erotic area. In fact, any form of abuse has a humiliating effect upon an individual's spirit because it makes him feel subject to another's power. The humiliated individual cannot hold his head up, which, as noted above, is the sign of a free and independent spirit. Bowing or lowering the head is also a sign of shame that is attached to the sexual nature of the body. Since sexuality cannot be denied, the feeling of humiliation associated with sexuality would be constantly present, which could drive anyone mad. Women burdened in this fashion suppress the humiliation by chronically tensing the muscles that lower the head. In time, these contracted muscles become a knot at the junction of neck and torso, which is commonly known as a widow's hump. This development is very rarely seen in men, in whom a strong feeling of humiliation would take the form of a shortened neck. Unlike women, men are rarely humiliated for sexual behavior and those who were humiliated by their mothers usually take it out on their wives.

Another feeling state relevant to this discussion is guilt. Guilt is strange because it has no particular bodily expression. It is what I have called a judgmental emotion.[3] The feeling of guilt is associated with a sense of having done something wrong. We constantly judge behavior as right or wrong, legal or criminal. One can be guilty of violating any acceptable code of behavior, but many people who commit crimes do not feel guilty, and many people feel guilty who have no idea that they have violated a rule of conduct. Obviously, the *feeling* of guilt must have a deeper base, a sense that something is wrong about one's self. We can get some understanding of this so-called feeling by considering the following: I invariably ask my patients if they feel any guilt about their sexuality, particularly about early masturbation. Many patients admit that they masturbated as young children, generally with feelings of guilt. Some, however, felt no guilt about that action despite the fact that their parents said it was bad. As one woman put it, "How could it be bad or wrong when it felt so good?" But if for any reason—say, fear or shame—it didn't feel so good, one could feel guilty.

In my view guilt is related to the overall feeling in the body. When one *feels* good about one's self, one cannot *feel* guilty about anything. By the same token, if a person has no feeling in his body, he cannot feel guilty, either. One will feel good when life or the spirit flows fully and freely through the body. When that is not the case because there are major tensions in the body limiting or breaking the individual's spirit, he will either feel bad or not let himself feel anything. In the former case, he will be aware of some guilt. That feeling of guilt will be related to the suppression of sexuality or anger. I have found that patients who feel guilty toward a parent lose their guilt when their anger against the parent is fully expressed in the therapy.

Feeling is the life of the body, just as thinking is the life of the mind. If a person can feel his tension not as a mysterious ache or pain but as a defense against certain impulses or feelings, his energy will be mobilized to release the tension and allow the appropriate expression of feeling. But this is no easy task. To know and to feel how much we have been hurt can be an enormous source of pain. Yet the only way to become free is to feel our tensions and sense their connection to suppressed feelings of fear, anger, and sadness. In many cases, becoming aware leads to the spontaneous expression of feeling and a resultant discharge of tension. Many patients have told me that they have spoken up quite spontaneously in painful situations, with positive results for the relationship at hand as well as for their self-esteem.

We suppress our feelings out of fear that we could not handle them if they arose. But this fear stems from our experience as children. We are adults now, neither helpless nor dependent and with a more mature understanding of life. However, some people need the support of a therapist to open up their deepest feelings. A person's suppressed anger may be so extreme as to be murderous, for example, and so he keeps it bottled up, not realizing that suppressed anger is like an explosive ready to blow up and damage innocent bystanders. To be aware of one's anger provides a measure of control and hence some safety. Many patients are also afraid of their sadness because it approaches despair. Suppressed crying, however, is a corrosive force that damages our internal organs, particularly the intestines. People who suffer from one form or another of colitis are, in my opinion, crying inwardly because they are afraid to cry outwardly.[4]

If we are to recover our grace and our health, we need to feel every part of our body. But as we have seen, many people have areas of the body they do not experience fully. We all know we have backs, for example, but few of us sense the tension in them or know whether they are supple or rigid. Often I have to demonstrate to a patient that it is possible to lie over the bioenergetic stool without pain because the back is—or should be—flexible. A back without feeling cannot perform all the functions of a supple, alive back. For example, the ability to back up a position or to back down when necessary depends on flexibility. The rigid person who literally cannot bend is also inflexible in his attitudes.

Any area of the body that is chronically tense and without feeling is a potential trouble spot that may break down. Tension in the neck or the lower back may result in collapsed vertebrae and ruptured disks. In some cases, the tension is so severe that deformities result, necessitating surgical intervention. These might have been prevented if the person were aware of his muscular tensions and the attitudes they represent.

The most important step toward improving health is to

ascertain how much feeling each part of the body has. The
following exercise will help you determine how much of your
body you feel. Keep in mind that the ability to feel the body
diminishes in most people as they move from head to foot.

EXERCISE 5.1

Do you feel your face? Are you aware of its expression? Do
you sense whether your mouth is tight or relaxed?
Can you feel any tension in your jaw? Can you move it freely
forward, backward, or to the side without pain?
Do you feel any tension in your neck? Can you move your
head freely, left and right, up and down?
Are your shoulders held tightly? Can you move them for-
ward, backward, and up and down easily?
Do you feel your back? Is it rigid or flexible?
Do you normally hold your chest in an inflated or deflated
position? Does your chest move freely when you breathe?
Is your diaphragm relaxed? Do you breathe abdominally?
Is your pelvis loose? Does it move when you walk? Do you
normally hold it in a forward or backward position?
Do you feel your backside touching the chair when you sit?
Do you feel your feet touching the ground when you stand
or walk? Do you normally feel your feet?

Another way I evaluate the amount of feeling in the body
is to ask patients to draw a figure of a man and a woman on
two separate sheets of paper. How complete the figures are and
how alive they look are an indication of how much patients feel
their bodies and where the feeling is located (fig. 5.3). For
example, some patients draw figures without hands or feet or

Figure 5.3. Drawings revealing feelings about the body. A segmented figure shows a feeling of disunity in the body and the lack of a sense of self, while a stick figure shows a lack of feeling, a sense of not having a body.

without eyes or any facial expression. Such figures clearly denote a lack of feeling in those areas. Other people draw stick figures, which denotes almost a total loss of body feeling. This is not to say that such people are immune to the prick of a pin, of course, but that they are unable to associate feelings such as sadness, joy, or fear with the body.

One set of feelings we have not discussed are the sexual feelings. In the next chapter, we will examine these feelings to determine their role in the grace and spirituality of the body.

6

Sexuality
and Spirituality

AS we have discussed in earlier chapters, many people believe that sexuality and spirituality are diametrically opposed. In their view, spirituality is something that goes on in the head, whereas sexuality takes place at the lower end of the body. This view distorts the reality of the human being, who is a sexually differentiated individual in every cell of his body. In a man, every cell has two Y chromosomes, in contrast to the cells in a woman's body, which have an X and a Y chromosome. Similarly, spirituality is a function of the whole body. Spirituality dissociated from sexuality becomes an abstraction, and sexuality dissociated from spirituality is a purely physical act. This dissociation is caused by the isolation of the heart, which severs the connection between the two ends of the body. When the feeling of love from the heart infuses the head, one senses one's connection to the universe and the universal. When it infuses the pelvis and legs, one feels connected to the earth and the particular. Moving upward, our spirit has a yang quality; moving downward, it has a yin quality. A basic bioenergetic principle states that the flow of excitation upward and down in the body is pulsatory, which means that it cannot extend more in one direction than the other. In terms of feeling, we cannot be more spiritual than we are sexual.

When our spirit enters fully into any act, that act takes on a spiritual quality due to the transcendence of the self. This transcendence can be experienced most vividly in the sexual act if it leads to the merger of two people in the dance of life. When this merger occurs, lovers transcend the boundaries of the self to become one with the larger forces in the universe.

Love is the key to such a merger. The closeness between a man and a woman is motivated by the same feeling of love that unites a mother and child, a person and his pet, man and his fellow man. Love is a state of pleasurable excitement that varies in intensity with the situation. The same kind of excitement occurs in the mystical union of a person and his god. Of course, the excitement that two lovers feel when they are close has an extra dimension, flowing downward through the body and strongly arousing the genital organs. When this occurs, the excitement and tension build to such a degree that the person feels an imperative urge for more intimate contact and for the discharge of the excitement. The joy of sex has two parts: (1) the pleasure a person derives from the excitement of contact and (2) the fulfillment provided by the genital discharge of the excitement. The initial pleasure is sensual and anticipatory; the pleasure of the orgastic release is purely sexual, and enormously satisfying. At the height of climax, it reaches the level of ecstasy.

For a few people, sex is a deeply moving experience in which the whole body participates and sexual excitement is intense. The surface of the body becomes charged, the eyes shine, and the skin is moist, warm, and glowing. The erogenous zones are also suffused with blood as the heart, sharing the excitement, drives the blood to the surface. When the lovers' eyes meet, a thrill of excitement electrifies the whole body. The desire for contact is very strong. If contact is made with a kiss, the body softens and melts, and one feels a sweet sensation of melting in the lower belly. At this point the genitals are charged with blood, but the charge is not overwhelming, for it is largely contained in the belly. The desire for a deeper, more intimate contact leads to intercourse. With penetration, there is a momentary lull before the rhythmic dance that leads to orgasm begins.

All of this happens spontaneously when two people are deeply in love. The individuals are moved to intercourse almost as if they were in a trance, although they are conscious of what they are doing. In the climax of full orgasm, however, they may nearly lose consciousness. The energetic discharge is so strong that the ego is overwhelmed by the feeling of release. The sense of merging between the two bodies can be so complete that the individuals feel as if they were one. At the same time, they may also feel as if they no longer inhabit their bodies.

After a strong orgastic discharge, a person feels deeply peaceful. Sleep can supervene before consciousness of the self returns. This dimming of consciousness is described by the French as *le petit mort*, the little death. One feels reborn after the experience.

In both the mystical and the orgastic experience, there is a sensing of communion with greater forces in the universe. But where the mystical experience is low-keyed and quiet, the orgastic experience is volcanic and earthshaking. In Hemingway's novel *For Whom the Bell Tolls*, the hero remarks after such an orgastic experience that he felt the earth move. In the mystical experience, a person relinquishes his self; in orgasm, the self is engulfed in a flood of energy and feeling. But to have such a powerful feeling, one needs to stay with the buildup of excitement until it explodes. This actually requires a strong self, since a weak self would be too frightened to risk the cataclysm. It is much like a ride on a roller coaster. To get the full excitement of the ride, one must keep one's eyes open and savor the dizzying rise and fall of the cars.

It is not generally appreciated that the act of intercourse was the inspiration for the primitive method of making a fire by twirling a stick rapidly in a groove to create the heat needed to ignite dry twigs and leaves. Friction → heat → flame is the sequence of both sets of actions, the goal of which is to produce a beautiful flame. Unfortunately, for most people the act of sex ends only in a few sparks, not in the flame that consumes the flesh, turning it into pure spirit. This is what transcendence is about.

Transcendence can also be achieved through acts that are nonsexual. We experience transcendence every time we are moved by a great passion or stirred by a great experience. In both cases the spirit becomes so charged that it overflows the boundaries of the self. When this happens, we no longer feel that we *have* a spirit but that we are *possessed* by it. Some religious examples of such possession include a voodoo ceremony I witnessed in Haiti in which an individual was driven into a trance while dancing to the continual and prolonged beating of drums; he then proceeded to eat fire, which seemed to have no effect on him. In the Sufi religion a state of trance is achieved through an extended, whirling dance. In the trance state the self is dissolved, and one experiences transcendence. When the Zen archer mentioned in chapter 3 stated, "It looses the shot," the 'it' was his spirit, which had taken full possession of his being and had directed the action. That was a truly transcendent experience.

Every creative act also has some degree of the transcendent in it. Two factors are needed to produce this transcendence: inspiration and passion. The inspiration for an artistic work always has some touch of the divine spirit, enabling the artist to surrender his ego and merge with his work. Through this surrender and merger, something new is born that is always bigger than the artist himself, whether it is a great painting or a great musical composition, containing a spirit that can move performers and audience deeply. Such creations seem to have a life of their own.

What greater creative act is there than the production of a new living being? Love, it is said, begins with a gleam in the eye and ends in the birth of a child. Seen in this light, the sexual act is the essence of creativity. While this is always true on a deep, biological level, one will not experience the mystery and grandeur of sex unless one is carried away by the divine passion of love.

Our inability to experience the orgastic response that leads to transcendence is due to the lack of passion in our lovemaking. Often, that passion was dampened early in life by painful experiences in both the oral and oedipal periods of development. The oral period refers to the first three years of life, when the infant's needs for nurturing, support, and loving contact are fulfilled by its mother. During this period its energy level is raised to the degree that passion is possible. Those needs can be met by the act of nursing, since that provides the most intimate, exciting, and fulfilling contact between mother and child. Most Westerners who have experienced this deeply satisfying sensation have had it for not more than nine months, as compared to the three or more years of breast-feeding that are common in underdeveloped countries and primitive societies.

If a child is weaned too soon, the loss of the breast can be experienced as the loss of its world, which can be heartbreaking. Such a loss, if reaffirmed by inappropriate parental responses during the oedipal period, can lead to the feeling "I will never have what I want, so why get excited? It will only end in pain."

A child will not be deprived of food or nurturing if he is not breast-fed. But babies need to feel the mother's body, to sense her life, and to absorb her energy. Contact with the mother's body stimulates a baby's breathing and increases its metabolism. If that contact is lost because the mother dies or becomes ill or depressed, the child is likely to be devastated. As we noted in an earlier chapter, the child armors against this pain by holding his breath and tensing his chest muscles. The effect is to limit his ability or inclination to reach out for love and to restrain his surrender to love when the possibility of a close attachment presents itself. In adulthood, sex is affected because it cannot be a wholehearted experience.

Another damaging effect on the child's excitement stems from parents' inability to tolerate the high level of energy in a child. They accuse him of being too demanding, too active, of wanting too much. They maintain that children should be seen and not heard. At three, many children have already suffered a marked loss of aliveness. I have seen so many children who look apathetic, whose eyes are dull and whose voices are weak, wheeled in a stroller by an indifferent mother or maid.

Passion and sexual responsiveness are further handicapped by events that occur during the initial flowering of sexual feeling in the oedipal period between the ages of three and six. In this period, a young boy is sexually attracted to his mother; a young girl, to her father. While the attraction is strong and exciting, the child has no desire for genital contact. In fact, such contact would be frightening to the child. In a healthy family setting, the sexual attraction dims as the child enters the so-called latency period and becomes more involved in the world outside the family. In an unhealthy setting, the parent encourages or reacts to the child's sexual interest. All too often, parents are seductive with their children, seeking an excitement from them that they do not get from their spouses. This adds an adult dimension to the relationship, introducing sexual feelings that are genitally oriented. These attract, frighten, and repel the child, who cannot withdraw because he is dependent on the parent's approval and support. Nor can he respond for fear of actual incest. Generally, any sexual response on the part of the child will subject him to condemnation and humiliation. Despite their own complicity, parents blame children for their sexual responses, projecting their own sexual guilt upon their offspring. In self-defense children cut off their sexual feelings, allowing them to retain love for their parents. In so doing, love is split off from sexual desire.

Like the suppression of any other feeling, the cutting off of sexual feelings is achieved by chronic muscular tension, which prevents feelings of excitement from entering the pelvis or the pelvis from moving if some excitement does break through. Anne was a good example of this problem. When I first saw her, she was an attractive woman in her early forties, unmarried but always involved sexually with some man. She was not depressed, but she sensed that she could not "get her act together," as the expression goes. To understand Anne, one had to look at her body, for it contained the story of her life. The two halves of her body looked different from each other. The lower half was full and heavy but radiated very little life and feeling. The upper half was narrow, with a better skin tone and more aliveness. She had full, well-shaped breasts, which made her feel womanly, and her eyes were big and had a soft, appealing look, which many men found attractive. She was seductive with men but not promiscuous. She would become sexually involved with various men, but despite her seeming warmth toward them, none of the men she had ever been attached to wanted to marry her.

The dysfunction between the two halves of Anne's body indicated that she had a split personality. One side of her acted independent and competent; in fact, she could support herself very well. I identified this side of her with the upper half of her body, which is largely under ego control. The other side of her personality was related to the passive, relatively lifeless lower half of her body. Although she had an active sexual life, she had very little sexual feeling and had never had an orgasm. A man's need or desire for her is what aroused her but never led to passion. This is a desperate condition for a woman, yet Anne did not seem desperate. In a group she was vivacious, well able to amuse people with her stories and jokes. It was only after some two years in therapy that she revealed the deep despair inside her, which she had consciously denied. Yet even from the start of therapy I could sense that Anne believed she could never get what she wanted. She had given up early on the wish to be married and have a family, and up until the time she entered therapy with me, she really had no idea what she wanted.

As the therapy progressed and she dropped the facade of acting carefree and open, she began to be depressed. Her low spirits did not stop her from working, but that activity seemed meaningless. During several months, she voiced the feeling that she would like to die—not that she thought of suicide but that her life appeared empty to her. This despair was a necessary step toward her recovery, for it forced her to become serious and face the reality of her being as expressed by her body.

Anne was a tragic figure. Her sexual activity was devoid both
of joy and of spirituality. Although she put on an act of moving
loosely and quickly she did not have a graceful body.

The heaviness in the lower half of Anne's body stemmed
from a holding against sexual excitement. The constriction in
her waist maintained this deadness by blocking the normal
downward flow of excitation. At the same time, her breathing
did not descend into her belly. Yet I could sense that she had
been a very lively little girl.

Sexual feelings are cut off when they are a source of pain,
humiliation, and danger, and Anne's experience was no excep-
tion. Early in her life she had become deeply attached to her
father, a strong tie that had lasted until his death two years
before she started therapy. She would do anything for him, an
attitude she later transferred to other men. He was equally
involved with her and very aware of her growing sexuality.
Although she was not aware of any overt sexual advances, she
recognized his sexual interest. She knew she excited him sexually, as her mother didn't. Although he kept control of his
actions, he felt guilty about his feelings, which he projected on
to her, labeling as "dirty" any manifestation of sexual feeling
in Anne. When she wanted to go out with boys her own age,
he called her a whore. He was conscious of how she dressed and
criticized her use of makeup. Yet he never hesitated to fool
around with other women or to make off-color remarks at
home. As a result, Anne viewed her own sexuality as "dirty,"
a feeling that located itself in the lower half of her body. She
had no choice but to dissociate herself from her sexuality,
recognizing at the same time this is what her father wanted
from her. By the time she reached adulthood, the habit of
keeping her sexuality under wraps was so deeply ingrained that
at times Anne felt hopeless about ever finding a man she could
fully love.

My task as her therapist was to help her bring life back into the lower half of her body. It was not an easy task, given the number of years that feeling had been cut off. The problem had to be approached both psychologically and physically. On the psychological level, Anne needed to gain an understanding of herself and her background. Physically, she needed to mobilize the lower half of her body so that she could feel it. Special exercises deepened her breathing, bringing her into contact with the sadness contained in her belly, a sadness she normally did not let herself feel. At the same time she began to cry, but only very slowly did she allow her crying to become deep. Anger was a feeling she had great difficulty mobilizing, largely because it was directed primarily against her father, who had used her but whom she loved and upon whom she felt dependent. She could not get angry at the men who also used her because she felt that she allowed it. This was a critical issue in her therapy, because there was no way for me to help Anne recover her sexual feelings unless she could feel herself to be a person and to have rights that she could assert and protect.

As the therapy progressed, Anne felt more strongly that she had suffered some sexual abuse by her father and by her brother. Just the realization that this could have happened broke the logjam in her personality. Now it was possible to mobilize her murderous rage. Breathing heavily and hitting the bed with a tennis racket, she voiced her anger with a force and outburst that I had not seen before. The fire was ignited in her being that could eventually flame into the passion of love.

Sexual seduction of a child by a parent is very common in this culture. When parents are unfulfilled in their relationship with each other, they turn to their children for affection, admiration, and sexual excitement. Sexual contact sometimes occurs, but more often the seduction takes the form of an intimacy in which the child is exposed to the parent's sexuality.

In too many homes, parents behave immodestly in front of young children in the mistaken belief that they are unaware of what is going on. The child, both stimulated and excited by a parent's sexual intimacy, is made to feel "special," which leads to the development of a narcissistic personality.[1] At the same time, the child is frightened by the possibility of incest and threatened by the jealousy and hostility of the parent of the same sex. To guard against these dangers, the child cuts off sexual excitement as in Anne's case. The situation in the home is compounded by a tendency in this culture to break down the barriers between adults and children in sexual matters, robbing the latter of their innocence. Some parents even take a perverse pride in the sexual sophistication of their children. Such children grow into adults who behave as if they feel superior but who harbor deep feelings of insecurity and inadequacy. In the sexual arena, a superficial sophistication covers an underlying anxiety and guilt about sexual feelings.

Sexual seduction, then, has a damaging effect on the child's personality, affecting both his body and his behavior. Heaviness and passivity of the lower part of the body, such as Anne developed, is only one form such damage may assume. Very commonly, especially in boys, sexual feeling is not fully cut off but held by muscular rigidity around the pelvis. In this case, the pelvis does not move freely, so that the person rarely reaches the phase of involuntary movement in which full orgastic release occurs. Genital excitement may be strong, but for many men it will end in a premature ejaculation because the rigidity of the pelvis limits its capacity to contain the charge until it can embrace the whole body. In severe cases, even erective potency can be affected.

Gracefulness is the mark of the truly sexual person. Gracefulness doesn't mean the ability to "rock" the pelvis, belly dance, or dive from a high board. It describes a body that is soft, in which there is a flow of excitation and a feeling of aliveness and pleasure in the ability to move. A sexual person doesn't swivel her hips while walking; instead, her pelvis moves freely, flowing with the whole body. When a person walks so that he feels each step touch the ground, the wave of excitation from his toes is coordinated with the respiratory wave, which, as we saw earlier, causes the pelvis to move with each breath. One sees this kind of walking more often in people in underdeveloped countries, who are not so dominated by their egos as Western people are. We in the Western world may be more sexually sophisticated, but these people are more sexually alive.

A body free from superego injunctions—be a good girl, obey your father and mother, don't raise your hand to your parent— is a body free from tension. It is an unspoken injunction in our culture that children must control their feelings. That injunction can be stated as "Don't lose your head, and don't let your feelings run away with you." Some self-control is positive, but when control becomes unconscious, it is maintained by chronic muscular tension and is a self-defeating process. In fact, the tension associated with the fear of losing one's head is responsible for arthritis in the cervical vertebrae and for tension headaches. A similar tension at the base of the spine where it joins the sacrum underlies most lower-back problems. This chronic tension, acting in concert with tension in the muscles, such as the quadriceps femoris, which joins the pelvis to the legs, immobilizes the pelvis so that it is unable to move spontaneously.

The immobilized pelvis is tipped either forward or back (see figs. 6.1A–C). In the normal state (Fig. 6.1A) the pelvis moves freely forward and back with the natural movement of the body and in harmony with the respiratory waves. As the wave descends into the pelvis with each expiration, it moves the pelvis forward. With inspiration, the pelvis moves backward. These

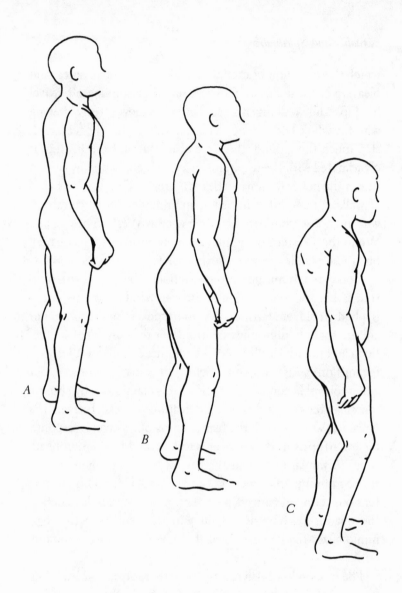

Figure 6.1. Pelvic position in response to tension.
(A) Normal pelvis held loosely.
(B) Pelvis cocked backward, exaggerating the concavity of the lower back.
(C) Pelvis locked forward, collapsing the back.

involuntary movements can be very slight when sitting; they become larger when walking. At the height of sexual excitement during climax, they become rapid and powerful. They do not occur if the pelvis is immobilized in one position or the other. In the backward position (fig. 6.1B), the pelvis is cocked and ready for action. The fixed backward position clearly denotes a holding back of sexual feeling. One finds this position more commonly in women, since it is to women that the injunction to hold back sexual feelings is more often directed. In men the more common disturbance is the forward position (fig. 6.1C) which has a pseudoaggressive meaning. Bringing the pelvis forward is a sexually aggressive movement, but since the pelvis is locked in this position, the appearance has no reality. The pelvis has to be pulled backward like the hammer of a gun before further forward movement is possible. When the pelvis is held forward, the back is rounded and collapsed and resembles the attitude of a dog with its tail between its legs.

If a person carries his pelvis in this position, it is often because he has been maltreated. Any form of physical abuse will undermine a person's natural cockiness, making him afraid and submissive, but one common form of punishment designed to achieve this effect is spanking. A child who is spanked will inevitably pull in his ass and contract his buttocks in response to pain. But the damage is more than physical. To be spanked is a humiliating experience that inflicts a severe narcissistic injury to the child's ego. In some cases, the child is even forced to assist in his own punishment by exposing the buttocks, bending over, lying on the parent's lap, or fetching the strap or the switch. In my view, there are other ways to discipline a child without resorting to this kind of sadistic punishment. Being spanked makes it very difficult to stand erect with pride or to walk with a loose and easy pelvis.

Most people are not aware that their pelvis is fixed. Often

they can move it so that it *looks* free, but when they are not making a conscious effort, it resumes its fixed position. In their sexual activity, people whose pelvises are kept forward have to push their sexual movements. Those who hold their pelvises in the backward position tend to restrain their movements.

Here is a simple exercise to help you sense where your pelvis is held.

EXERCISE 6.1

Stand in front of a mirror so that you can see your back when you turn your head. Does your back look straight, is your head held up, is your pelvis back? Now make sure that your feet are parallel and about six inches apart; then push your pelvis fully forward. Can you see or sense how your back rounds up or bends, causing you to lose height? Bring the pelvis backward slowly. Can you see the straightening of your back? What feeling is associated with each position? Which is your habitual pose?

Now, as you stand, bend your knees slightly and try to let your pelvis hang loosely so that it can move freely like the hand on the wrist. Breathe deeply and slowly, trying to feel the respiratory wave go deep into the pelvis. Can you sense any movement in that structure? How does it feel? Can you sense any anxiety in that movement? For the reasons mentioned above, it does not occur in most people.

As we have seen, sexual responsiveness is affected by tension in any part of the body. But the ability to surrender to orgasm is particularly affected by tension in the pelvic floor. In most people the pelvic floor is tight out of an unconscious fear that relaxing it might result in an undesired discharge. This fear stems from early toilet-training experiences. When training occurs before the age of two and a half years, the child uses the muscles of the pelvic floor and the buttocks to control the excretory function, since the external anal sphincter does not become operative until that age. Even after the external anal sphincter becomes functional, the fear persists and extends later to orgasm. One cannot allow the sexual discharge to occur fully and freely because it requires surrendering one's hard-won control. The earlier a child is trained, the greater the tension in the pelvic floor. As a result, such training often results in bowel disturbances. If parents react with the use of enemas or suppositories, a child's problem is increased by the invasion and violation of his body. I have treated two women who were toilet trained by nine months of age and who, in consequence, suffered nearly a complete loss of feeling in the pelvis and pelvic floor.

A double set of sphincter muscles surrounds the anus. The internal sphincter, which is not under conscious control, stays closed until fecal matter accumulates and fills the rectum. Until that point, the external sphincter remains open and relaxed. When the rectum fills up and one has the urge to defecate, the internal sphincter relaxes, while the external sphincter closes tightly until one is in a position to evacuate properly. This means that in the absence of an urge to defecate we can afford to keep the pelvic floor relaxed and the external sphincter open, but many people are frightened that letting go the sexual discharge could result in soiling themselves. In some cases, this fear is generalized into a pervasive anxiety that "the bottom will fall out," as if a catastrophe—or an accident—were just around the corner.

Actually, all fears affect the pelvic floor. A sudden fright will cause a sharp contraction. Suppressed fear, on the other hand, will cause chronic tension. But if we are unaware of the fear, we will not feel the tension.

To relax the pelvic floor, we must first become aware of the extent to which we hold it up. The following exercise can help you become aware of pelvic tension.

EXERCISE 6.2

Stand with your feet parallel and about eight inches apart, your knees slightly bent and your weight forward. Let the pelvis drop backward, as described in the previous exercise. Try to push down the pelvic floor while breathing deeply into the abdomen. At the same time, try to open the anal sphincter as if you would let some gas out. (Nothing will come out unless you are holding something in. I have conducted this exercise in my classes over many years, and no one has suffered an embarrassing experience.)

Then, deliberately pull up the anus and pelvic floor by squeezing the ass. Can you feel tension develop? Now try to let the pelvic floor down. Does it feel more relaxed? Repeat this exercise several times to really learn the difference between a tense pelvic floor and a relaxed one.

To become more aware of how you hold the pelvic floor during your normal activities, repeat this exercise a number of times during the day while walking, sitting at a desk, or engaged in any activity. You may need to pay a good deal of attention to the area before you can keep it fully relaxed, but the effort will yield a rich reward in increased sexual feeling.

Because sex, like defecation and urination, is one of the functions most closely associated with our animal nature, it may be difficult to accept the connection between spirituality and sexuality. If we don't see the connection, it is because we have lost touch with that which unites them—the heart of the body. When we love our sexual partner with all the love in our hearts, the embrace is spiritual as well as sexual. When we embrace God with the love of our bodies, the contact is sexual as well as spiritual. This notion may sound heretical, but sexual activity has long been used in the religious rites of primitive cultures to touch the godhead. Even in the Judeo-Christian tradition, dancing has been part of many religious ceremonies. Whatever means are used to establish a feeling connection to the infinite, it must involve the body if it is to be more than an idea in one's head. All religions recognize that a man must surrender his ego if he is to become one with his god. There is no better or more direct way to experience this surrender than in the act of sexual love.

The next chapter will discuss the conditions that allow a person to achieve this transcendence. This state is called grounding.

7

Grounding: The Connection to Reality

THE quality of an individual's sexual feeling depends on the amount of energy or excitation in his body, for diminished energy means decreased feeling. It depends also on the degree of gracefulness in the body, which allows the body's energetic charge to flow freely and fully. Finally, it depends on how grounded the individual is, how connected he is energetically to the earth. If an energetic system (an electrical circuit, for example) is not grounded, then there is the risk that an extra-strong charge would overwhelm and blow the system. In the same way, individuals who are not grounded risk being overwhelmed by strong feelings, sexual and otherwise. To prevent this from happening, ungrounded individuals must reduce all feelings, for should they become overwhelmed, they become terrified. By contrast, a grounded individual can support a strong excitation, which he will experience as joy and transcendence.

We humans are like trees, rooted in the ground at one end and reaching to heaven at the other. The extent of our reach depends on the strength of our root system. Uproot a tree and the leaves die; uproot a person and his spirituality becomes a lifeless abstraction.

Some may argue that people do not have roots like trees. However, as creatures of the earth, we are connected to the ground through our legs and feet. If the connection is vital, we say that a person is *grounded*. The same term describes the connection of an electrical conductor with the earth to prevent an overcharge in an electrical system. We use the term in bioenergetics to describe a person's connection to the earth, his fundamental reality. When we say that a person is well grounded or that he has his feet solidly on the ground, it means that he knows who he is and where he stands. To be grounded is to be connected to the basic realities of life: one's body, one's sexuality, the people with whom one has relationships. One is connected to these realities to the extent that one is connected to the earth.

In evaluating an individual's personality, it is important to see how he stands and how well connected he is to the ground. This is a common procedure in bioenergetic analysis. If a person has a strong and secure sense of himself, he will naturally stand erect. If he is frightened, he will tend to cower. If he is sad or depressed, his body will droop. If he is trying to deny or compensate for inner feelings of insecurity, he will stand like a martinet, and his posture will be unnaturally rigid.

In addition to its psychological meaning, the way a person stands also has sociological significance. When we say that a person has standing in the community, we mean that he is recognized as somebody. We expect a king to stand regally, a servant to stand humbly, and a fighter to stand loosely on the balls of his feet as an expression of his readiness for action. We know that a person of character will stand up for his beliefs regardless of the situation.

We also know that some adults, despite their chronological age, are unable to stand on their own two feet. What we mean is that such people are dependent upon others for support. The absence of feeling in their legs makes their contact with the ground mechanical. A table has legs on which it rests, but we would never think of it as grounded. Of course, unlike inanimate objects, people always have some degree of feeling in their legs. For some, however, the feelings are not strong enough to reach consciousness unless attention is focused on the body. It is not enough simply to know that one's feet are on the ground. What is required is an energetic process in which a wave of excitation passes downward through the body and into the legs and feet. Feeling grounded occurs when the wave of excitation reaches the ground, reverses direction, and flows upward, as if the earth were pushing back to hold us up. Standing this way, we can consciously hold our ground.

When we speak of a person as up in the air, we don't mean that his feet are literally off the ground but that he pays more attention to his thoughts—or, more likely, his daydreams—than to putting one foot in front of the other. He knows where he is going, but he may be so preoccupied with what he will do when he gets there that the act of walking is automatic. He can get so lost in a daydream that he isn't even aware that he is walking. Since we humans think almost all the time while awake, one may wonder if a distracted air isn't the natural way. But normally attention oscillates rapidly enough that it is possible to be aware of what is going on in the mind and in the body simultaneously. I have made it a practice when giving lectures to pause frequently to check my state of tension and my breathing and to feel my feet on the floor. My listeners welcome the interruption because it gives them time to breathe, just as it gives me time to collect myself. Invariably the success of my presentation is directly proportional to the degree to which I am in contact with my body and my feelings. The success of this practice depends on the presence in the body of a strong energetic pulsation that connects both ends of the body. When that connection is broken so that the person is not grounded, the conscious attempt to shift one's attention produces an awkward and disturbing break in the connection between the speaker and his audience. I have worked with my body bioenergetically for a long time to achieve some solid grounding.

The quality of a person's grounding determines his inner sense of security. If he is well grounded, he feels secure on his legs and certain that the ground is "there" for him. It is not a question of how strong his legs are but how much feeling they have. Strong, heavy legs may seem especially well suited to supporting a person, but all too often they function mechanically. Such legs betray a basic insecurity in the individual that the heavy muscular development is intended to overcome. A similar lack of security is found in people whose legs are underdeveloped but whose shoulders are big and strong. Unconsciously fearful of falling or being left, such individuals hold themselves up by their shoulders instead of looking to the ground for support. Such a posture places an enormous stress on the body and so perpetuates any underlying insecurity.

A person's basic feeling of security is determined by his early relationship with his mother. Positive experiences—loving care, support, affection, approval—leave the child's body in a soft, natural, and graceful state. The child experiences his body as a source of pleasure and joy, identifying with it and feeling connected to his animal nature. Such a child will grow up well grounded, with a strong inner sense of security. On the other hand, when a child experiences a lack of loving support from his mother, his body stiffens. Stiffening is a natural reaction both to a physical chill and to an emotional coldness. Any coldness in a mother undermines her child's sense of security by breaking his connection to his primary reality. A mother is our personal earth, just as the earth is our universal mother. Any insecurity a child feels in relation to his mother will become structured in his body. Unconsciously, the child will tense his diaphragm, hold his breath, and raise his shoulders out of fear. Once the insecurity becomes structured in the body, he is caught in a vicious circle, since he will continue to feel undermined long after he ceases to depend on his mother.

The problem of insecurity is insoluble if a person is not aware of his lack of grounding. He may believe he is secure because he has money, position, and a family, but he will lack an inner feeling of security unless he is grounded.

The clearest indication of a lack of grounding is standing with locked knees, a position that rigidifies the legs and limits feeling in them. Such a stance also prevents the knees from acting as shock absorbers for the body. Like the shock absorbers in a car, the knees bend when the body is under stress, allowing the stress to pass through the leg and into the ground (see figs. 7.1A and B). As figure 7.1C shows, locked knees trap stressful pressure in the lower back. Most of us don't realize that psychological pressures act on the body just like physical forces. If we lock our knees to support these pressures, we leave our backs vulnerable to serious injury.

Standing with your knees slightly bent may be uncomfortable if you are not used to it. If your muscles tire, instead of locking your knees, sit down and rest to relieve the fatigue. Locking the knees may take away the pain, but only because the legs rigidify and lose all feeling. People who have learned to stand correctly usually find that it makes a dramatic difference in the way they experience their body. "When you unlocked my knees, you unlocked my energy," a reader once wrote me. For this reason, it is standard practice in bioener-

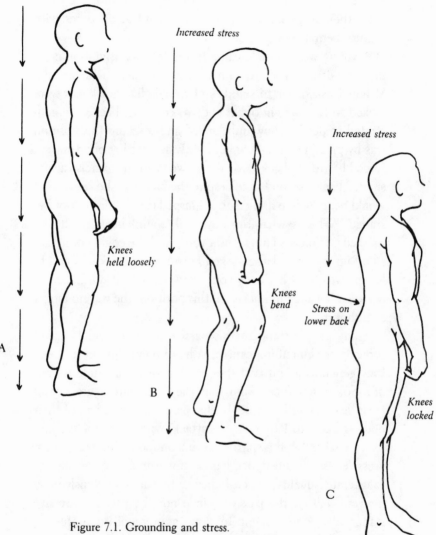

Normal stress of gravity

Increased stress

Increased stress

Knees
held loosely

Knees
bend

Stress on
lower back

A

B

C

Knees
locked

Figure 7.1. Grounding and stress.
*(A) With the knees held loosely, a person stands straight and
tall.*
*(B) When stress increases from physical exertion or emo-
tional burdens, the knees bend to absorb it.*
*(C) If the knees are locked and unable to absorb stress, the
stress hits the lower back and bends the upper body forward.*

getic therapy to insist that patients stand at all times with slightly bent knees.

A young woman once came to me for a consultation complaining of a lack of fulfillment and satisfaction in her life. When I asked her to stand, I observed that her knees were locked and the weight of her body was over her heels. I demonstrated to her just how unbalanced and insecure this position was by pressing a single finger lightly against her chest, which forced her to fall backward. When we tried the exercise again, she fell back a second time despite the fact that she knew what would happen. She immediately grasped the significance of her stance. "This is what the boys call 'round heels,'" she remarked. "It means I am a pushover." And she could not in fact stand up to them. I then asked her to bend her knees and to let the weight of her body come forward until it was balanced between her toes and heels. In this position, she was no longer a pushover.

Many people stand in this passive position, which makes forward movement impossible. When I point this out to them, they generally admit that they have a passive attitude toward life. Some, however, claim that they are quite aggressive in their dealings with people. In that case, the upper half of their body is likely to look ready to attack, whereas the lower half looks passive. Such a split is not uncommon. Because the aggressiveness of the upper half is unnatural, it often has an exaggerated quality, which indicates that it is a defensive maneuver. Neither the passive stance nor the pseudoaggressive stance allows movement to flow, a prerequisite to feeling grounded. Free movement is possible only if one stands with knees slightly bent and weight forward—a naturally aggressive position.

The following exercise will help you evaluate your own stance:

EXERCISE 7.1

Stand in the basic position, feet parallel, knees slightly bent, pelvis loose and slightly retracted. Now let the upper half of your body lean forward until you feel your weight on the balls of your feet. You may feel that you will fall flat on your face, but if you lose your balance, you will simply step forward. You will not lose your balance if your head is properly aligned.

Bring your head up so that you look straight ahead. To balance your weight, imagine carrying a basket on your head.

Then, with your head held high, let your chest collapse and your belly expand so that your breathing is full and deep. Let the ground hold you up.

You may not find this posture comfortable at first. In fact, you may feel some pain from tense muscles being stretched. As these muscles relax, the pain will eventually disappear. Bear with it. There is no need to be afraid of the pain of growth, especially when your goal is to let the life in your body flow freely.

It is from this position that one is launched most gracefully into motion. Unlocked knees translate into a springier step, which in turn helps one feel more grounded.

EXERCISE 7.2

While walking, make a deliberate effort to feel your feet touch the ground with each step by walking slowly and allowing your weight to rest on each foot. Let your shoulders relax and make sure that you are not holding your breath or locking your knees.

Do you sense a lowering of your body's center of gravity? Do you feel more in contact with the ground, more relaxed, more secure? This way of walking may feel strange to you at first. If it does, realize that under the pressure of modern living, you have lost the natural gracefulness of your body.

Walk slowly at the outset to promote feeling in your feet and legs. Once you have a good sense of the ground, you may vary your rhythm to suit your mood.

As a result of this exercise, do you feel more in touch with your body? Do you spend less time lost in thought while walking? Do you feel freer, looser?

Paying attention to the way one walks is only the first step toward the recovery of grace. One also needs to soften the legs and to allow more feeling and sensation to develop in them. The following exercise is one I have my patients perform regularly both in therapy and at home. Called the basic grounding exercise, it was first described in my book of bioenergetic exercises, *The Way to Vibrant Health.* [1] Because of its importance, it is included again here.

EXERCISE 7.3

With your feel parallel and about eighteen inches apart, bend forward and touch the ground with the fingertips of both hands, bending the knees as much as necessary to accomplish this. Allow the weight of the body to rest on the balls of the feet, not on the hands or the heels. Keeping the fingertips on the ground, slowly straighten the knees but do not *lock* them. Hold this position for about twenty-five breaths, breathing easily and deeply. You may sense your legs begin to vibrate, which indicates that waves of excitation are beginning to flow.

If vibration does not occur, it is a sign that the legs are too tense. In that case, some vibratory activity can be induced by slowly bending and straightening the legs repeatedly. But the bending and straightening should be minimal, just enough to keep the knees soft. You should do this exercise for at least twenty-five breaths or until the vibratory activity starts. You may also notice that your breathing becomes deeper and more spontaneous.

When you resume your standing position, keep your knees slightly bent, your feet parallel, and your weight forward. Your legs may continue to vibrate, which is a sign of life. Do you have more feeling in your legs? Do you feel your feet resting on the ground? Do you feel more relaxed?

If your legs don't vibrate in this position, you can extend the time of the exercise to sixty breaths and practice it several times a day. (Another way to induce vibrations in the legs is to stand on one leg in the position described above while raising the other off the ground. This increases the charge in the standing leg.) This basic grounding exercise promotes a sense of letting down or relaxing. Many years ago, while teaching bioenergetic concepts to a group of psychologists at Esalen Institute, I demonstrated it to a young woman who was a dancer and the resident t'ai chi ch'uan instructor. When her legs began to vibrate, she remarked, "I've been *on* my legs all my life, but this is the first time I've ever been *in* them." If an individual becomes overexcited during bioenergetic therapy, this exercise will restore his or her self-control. One of my patients, a musical-comedy actor, used to practice it while waiting in the wings to be auditioned for a role. While his fellow singers vocalized and practiced singing, he would assume the grounding position and get his legs vibrating. He relates that most of his competitors became so tense during the audition that their voices failed under the strain. In contrast, he felt relaxed and often got the part. I myself have consistently performed this exercise for about thirty-four years, and I still do it every morning to keep my legs soft and relaxed. That may not seem so important for a young person, but it is imperative if one wishes to retain some gracefulness as one grows older. Age affects a person's legs more than it does any other part of the body. In fact, it is fair to say that a person is only as young as his legs.

Squatting is another exercise that promotes the feeling of being grounded, for it brings one as close to the ground as possible without lying on it. Children easily assume this position, as do primitive people and those living in underdeveloped countries. But most Western people find it almost impossible to squat without falling backward. They may hold the position for a short time by leaning against or holding on to a support. The inability to maintain a squatting position unassisted is due to the inordinate tension most people have in their thighs, buttocks, and lower back. Practicing squatting is highly recommended for people with these problems.

EXERCISE 7.4

The feet should be parallel and about eight inches apart. Try to squat and hold the position, keeping the legs and feet parallel without using any support. However, if some support is needed, hold on to a piece of heavy furniture in front of you. The correct position of the squat requires the heels to be on the ground and the weight of the body to be on the balls of the feet.

If you need some support, another way to do this exercise is to place a rolled-up towel under your heels while squatting. The roll should be just big enough to enable you to maintain the position. It should not be comfortable, for that defeats the purpose of the exercise, which is to stretch the contracted muscles of the legs. You can promote this purpose by rocking on your feet, shifting your weight forward and backward.

If squatting becomes painful, come down on the knees, extend your legs backward, and sit on your heels. This, too, may be painful if your ankles and feet are tight. If that is the case, resume squatting to loosen the ankles. Alternating these positions promotes the process of letting down.

It is important to repeat here that a graceful movement starts from the feet and the ground. Having done the grounding exercises described above, one can experience this principle more vividly through the following exercise, which duplicates one of the most common actions we take each day: getting up from a chair.

EXERCISE 7.5

Sit in a straight-backed chair with both feet on the floor. You will rise from that sitting position by pushing yourself up from the ground rather than by lifting yourself out of the chair. To do the former you must shift your weight on to the balls of your feet. Now press down against the floor and push yourself up straight. In doing so, you have made a very strong contact with the ground. Now repeat the exercise, but this time lift yourself out of the chair as you would normally do.

Can you feel the difference between the two ways of getting up? Repeat the exercise two or three times until the difference is evident. When you push yourself up, you use your legs fully. In lifting, the upper part of the body is more involved, and more effort is needed.

In addition to relaxed muscles, proper alignment is essential for the full and free flow of excitation in the body. Such alignment begins in the foot, where the arch acts like a spring mechanism to absorb the shocks of walking. If a person is well grounded, every time he takes a step, his arch will flatten a little as the weight shifts to the other foot. Obviously, a person cannot be grounded if his arches are so high that his feet fail to make full contact with the earth or if his arches have lost their elasticity and fallen. Flat feet cause a loss of spring in the step. Collapsed arches mean that the feet are undercharged and overstressed. Overweight people tend to have flat feet, as does anyone laboring under a heavy emotional or physical burden. High arches, on the other hand, are seen most often in individuals with birdlike legs. Raised by unavailable or un-pleasant mothers, such people feel obliged to hold themselves up from the ground.

The position of the feet themselves is also important to proper alignment. It is rare in our culture to see people who stand or walk with their feet facing forward. Most people walk with their feet turned out to some degree. This position shifts the weight of the body to the heels and the pressure wave to the lateral aspects of the legs. Combined with flat feet, this position can cause serious damage to the body, as a physician friend reported in a letter. "I am still overweight and my knees and feet are suffering from the years of tension and being out of alignment," he wrote. "The lateral aspects of my knee cartilages are worn down to the bone and I can-not be on my legs for very long. I asked the orthopedist how this condition could have happened and he guessed that my flat feet from early childhood threw most of the stress of the knee joint on the outer aspect, which is now worn down, a condition which cannot be corrected. So I am, as always, un-gainly on my feet." This sad story could have been prevented by exercises. One should learn to stand with the feet parallel and about eight inches apart and the knees slightly bent and in line with the middle of each foot. If one also suffers from flat feet, one should press on the outside edge of each foot, keeping the knees positioned as described above. The legs may begin to shake, which indicates that tension is being released.

Standing or walking with the feet turned out in a *V* position may also be the result of chronic tension in the the gluteal muscles. In most cases, this tension develops as a result of too early toilet training, which produces a "tight ass" and a V-shaped walk. The following exercise reproduces the effect of this tension on the body:

EXERCISE 7.6

Stand with feet about eight inches apart and absolutely paral-lel. Keep the knees slightly bent and the weight forward. Place one hand on the pelvic floor under the anus. Now bring the heels together so that the feet form a *V*. Can you feel the ass tighten and close up?

Now walk with your feet in the *V* position and note how ungraceful the movement is. Next, take some steps with the feet parallel. Do you sense a significant difference in the quality of your movements? Observe how other people walk. Do you see the difference between those whose feet are parallel and those whose feet are turned out?

The following exercise is designed simply to relax the feet. Used just before retiring, this exercise has helped chronic in-somniacs fall asleep by reducing the charge in the head.

EXERCISE 7.7

Stand with one or both feet on a one-inch wooden dowel or broom handle. As in the other exercises, your feet should be bare to promote feeling in them. You can shift them so that the pressure of the dowel is on the ball of the foot, the arch, or near the heel. If the exercise hurts, reduce the weight on the foot.

Do you have more feeling in your feet after this exercise? Are you more in contact with the ground than before? Can you sense a difference in the state of relaxation of your body?

Valuable as these bioenergetic exercises are in helping a person feel his feet firmly on the ground, a continuing awareness of the body is necessary to achieve significant changes in feelings and behavior. Thus, it is important to be aware of one's legs and feet whether one is walking, standing, or sitting. When sitting, it is also important to be aware of the seat of one's pants. Most people slump in a chair so that the weight of the body is centered on the sacrum and coccyx rather than on the ischial tuberosities in the buttocks. While this may seem like a relaxed and comfortable position, it represents some degree of withdrawal into the self, not unlike a child curling up in a corner to isolate and protect himself from the world. There is no real security in this position because one is unprepared to deal with adult realities. To sit in a grounded position, one must feel the buttocks making contact with the seat of the chair. This keeps the back straight and the head directed forward.

A therapist often sits face-to-face with a patient to discuss the latter's problems and feelings. I have found that these discussions are more direct and fruitful when my patient and I sit in the grounded position. Contact between us is facilitated when each looks more directly into the other's eyes. This sense of being seen and connected adds a spiritual element to the therapy. By reducing anxiety and increasing a feeling of security, it also has a positive effect in any situation where people sit and talk to each other. It is invaluable in a crisis such as I experienced flying in a small single-engine seaplane when we encountered gale conditions. I was able to avoid the panic that touched some of the other passengers by focusing on feeling my bottom solidly in the seat and breathing easily and deeply.

Because lower back pain is so common, some people maintain that man was never intended to stand erect. But if lower back trouble were due to a fault of nature, every one of us would suffer from this disorder. When one studies the stance of different people from a bioenergetic point of view, it becomes clear that it is those who are ungrounded who suffer from lower back problems. Those who are grounded and graceful are held erect by a vital force that moves upward from the ground through the feet, legs, thighs, pelvis, back, neck, and head. The existence of this vital force or energy is recognized in Yoga, where it is called kundalini and said to flow from the sacrum to the head along the backbone as the Yoga disciple meditates in the lotus position. Standing or walking, one experiences this energetic movement as coming from the ground. Whatever the position, such a flow of energy is possible only if one is grounded. Some people have this quality naturally. According to Lee Strasberg, the well-known acting teacher Eleonora Duse "had a strange way of smiling. It seemed to come from her toes. It seemed to move through the body and arrive at the face and mouth."[2]

In considering man's erect posture, it is useful to return again to the image of a tree. The ability of a tree to maintain its upright position depends more on the strength of its roots than on the rigidity of its structure. In fact, the more rigid the structure, the more vulnerable the tree is to being uprooted in a storm. The roots are important not only in acting as a support system but in obtaining the necessary nutrients from the ground for the growth of the tree. Sap carrying these nutrients upward to the leaves is essential to the life of a tree. But the sap must also flow downward after it has been charged by the sun's energy. Similarly, the vital energetic flow in man is both up and down.

The human organism is vastly different from a tree, but almost all life is alike in that it exists at the interface where the earth and sky meet. It is here that the energy of the sun transforms the matter of earth into protoplasm. Like trees, we humans look to the heavens as the source of life-giving energy, but we also depend on the earth for our very substance. Only angels are free from this dependence on the earth, because they are neither animal nor vegetable. Unfortunately, humans can't be animal and angel at the same time. If we dissociate from our animal nature (and the lower half of the body), we lose our grounding. To be grounded one has to be a sexual person. But as we discussed in chapter 6, to be a sexual adult, one's pelvic movements must be free.

These movements are voluntary during the preorgastic phase and involuntary during orgasm. The latter are deeply pleasurable, but voluntary movements can be pleasurable as well if they are not pushed or forced. Any deliberate forcing creates tension. In general, our movements are graceful only if we allow the wave of excitation to flow upward, unimpeded, from the ground. A relaxed pelvis is instrumental in this. If we push it forward in walking or in sex, the muscles around the pelvis contract, reducing sensation. It is far better to allow the pelvis to reach forward from below on its own.

In chapter 6, we had an exercise designed to measure constricting tension in the pelvis. Now, incorporating the concept of grounding, we can attempt some exercises that can actually help the pelvis move freely.

EXERCISE 7.8

Stand with your feet parallel and about eight inches apart.
Bend the knees slightly. Lean forward and press down on the
balls of the feet. Do you feel you are being propelled forward?
We walk this way, except that we press down with one foot at
a time.

Now bend the knees more and press down again on the balls
of the feet. This time do not let the heels come off the floor.
Did the reactive force move upward, straightening your knees?

Repeat the above maneuver a third time, keeping your knees
bent and your heels on the ground. This time lean forward and
keep your pelvis loose. Did you feel the pelvis moving forward?

I have found that most people have difficulty with this exercise because they cannot press down on the ground without
tensing their legs. If one is grounded, the exercise is easy to do.
Here is another exercise that aims at the same result, namely
sensing how the pelvis can move from below rather than from
above. This exercise is also difficult, but with practice one can
free up the lower part of the body to the extent that it becomes
much more than a mechanical conveyance. When the pelvis
moves freely, one feels uplifted, graceful, and at ease.

EXERCISE 7.9

Stand with the feet parallel and about twelve inches apart.
The knees should be bent slightly and the hands placed on
them. The objective is to move the pelvis from side to side using
only the legs and feet. The upper part of the body should be
relaxed and inactive.

Press down on the ball of the right foot, straighten the right knee, and let the pelvis swing to the right. You accomplish this by twisting the muscles in the right leg. Then shift your weight onto the left foot, press down, and straighten the left knee slightly. You should feel the pelvis move to the left. Then shift to the right leg and repeat the maneuver, trying to get the pelvis to move to the right without engaging the upper part of the body. Continue the exercise, using each leg in turn about five times.

Most people can move the pelvis by twisting the upper part of the body, but since this movement is not connected to the ground, it lacks grace and does not provide any pleasure. The grounded movement is exciting, while the forced movement is mechanical.

This exercise is similar to the basic movement of the traditional Hawaiian hula dance. When done by Hawaiians, the dance looks easy and graceful. But most Western people look extremely awkward doing it because their bodies are too rigid and they have no feeling of how to move from the ground. Pelvic movements that are not grounded may look sexy and seem exciting, but it is a sexuality divorced from feeling. When grounded, such movements have a spiritual quality, which explains their use in the rites of ancient religions.

One may wonder how the principle of grounding applies to the act of intercourse when two people are lying on top of each other in bed. If the man is on top, he can ground himself by pressing his feet against the footboard of the bed or against a wall. With the knees bent, the pelvis will move naturally. In the absence of a footboard or an available wall, he may dig his toes into the mattress so that the pelvic movement starts in the feet. If the woman is on the bottom, she may ground herself by pressing her feet into the mattress or by wrapping her legs around her partner so that his body becomes her ground. (Of course, the partners may also reverse positions.) Applying this principle to the sexual movements of intercourse can make a significant difference in the quality and intensity of the sensations. Excitation is increased because the whole lower part of the body is actively engaged in the sexual act, not just the genital apparatus. Because the pelvis moves more freely, there is more feeling in the pelvic area. If one is grounded in the sexual act, it is easier to surrender to the orgastic release.

Purely from the point of view of medical health, grounding is of inestimable value. It has an immediately beneficial effect on high blood pressure. Coupled with deeper breathing, the grounding exercises significantly lower systolic pressure and even have some effect in reducing diastolic pressure. Of course, these reductions will not be permanent unless the person makes a noticeable change in his relationship to the ground he stands on, his body, his sexuality, and his relationships. In bioenergetic therapy one looks for that change to be manifest physically. When therapy is successful, a patient's feet actually become larger, while his legs soften, his pelvis loosens, his breathing deepens, and his shoulders drop. Once he is grounded, a person no longer holds himself up but allows the ground to support him. By coming down to earth, he finds his blood pressure also drops. But effecting that kind of change requires a commitment to the body and to a way of life that respects the body and its needs.

Unfortunately, our culture is moving away from the body as the source of feeling and spirituality. Our fitness programs are not designed to enhance the sensitivity of the body but to hone it as if it were a machine. In so doing, they produce people who are fit only to run the race of life. I suppose that if reaching the top is one's goal in life, our modern-day fitness programs may help. But if one's goal is to experience the joy of being fully alive, the excitement of feeling part of this pulsating universe, and the deep satisfaction of being a person who is both graceful and gracious, one must turn elsewhere.

When I was a young man, being "earthy" was regarded as a virtue. I never hear anyone described that way anymore. Has the quality of having one's feet on the ground lost its meaning? I believe it has. The modern individual is more properly described as "flying high and fast." It is hard to slow down when the world is racing by. It is difficult to be grounded when the culture itself is ungrounded, when it denies reality and promotes the illusion that success represents a higher state of being and successful people live richer and more fulfilling lives. All the same, the real values in life are "earthy" values: health, gracefulness, connectedness, pleasure, and love. But these values have meaning only if one's feet are planted firmly on the ground.

8

The Structural Dynamics of the Body

THE human body is balanced energetically and structurally. It is also balanced chemically by a process known as homeostasis that maintains the acidity of the blood at a constant level. Energetically, it is balanced between two opposing forces, one acting from above to draw the organism upward and one acting from below to pull it downward. Again, the example of the tree is appropriate; its branches grow upward toward the sun, while its roots extend into the earth. In Chinese thinking, these two forces, known as yin and yang, represent the energy of the earth and of the sun, respectively. The roots of a plant absorb yin energy from the earth, and the leaves absorb yang energy from the sun. In the Tao, yin and yang lie side by side in harmony. But life is not static; it is in constant flux due to the interaction of these two forces, seemingly engaged in a constant tug-of-war. Harmony is like the midpoint of the swing of the pendulum that exists only in the moment when the movement changes direction.

Life developed at the surface of the earth where the energy from the sun interacted and united with the energy from the earth. The union of opposites to create life is the principle of sexual reproduction. For the Chinese, these opposites are sexually oriented, with yin equated with the feminine and yang with the masculine. To understand this interaction between opposing energetic forces, we need Reich's concept of superimposition, in which two energetic waves spin around each other in a creative action.[1] That process is represented diagramatically in figure 8.1.

In the course of evolution, the energy level of some organisms increased greatly, with the result that in the higher animals the charge at both ends of the body became strong enough to form two centers. The upper center became the brain; the lower became the sexual and reproductive system. The middle center of activity became the heart, from which

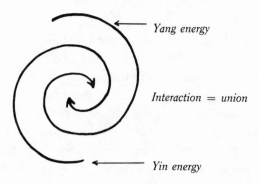

Figure 8.1. Reich's concept of superimposition.

blood pumped to both ends of the body connects them ener-getically to the center (see fig. 8.2). In a tree, that connection is made by the upward and downward flow of sap. As we saw in chapter 2, the movement of fluid is related to and dependent on a corresponding energy flow in the form of waves of excita-tion that traverse the organism. In the human body these waves of excitation are the force that maintains its erect posture. In general, these waves are stronger during daytime periods of activity than during nighttime periods of rest.

It is a basic rule of bioenergetics that energy charge cannot exceed energy discharge. Although it is possible to eat more food than one needs for the production of energy at a given time, the excess will be stored as fat, ready to be converted into energy when needed. Similarly, if one is in dire straits—for example, in the midst of a famine—one may expend more energy than one takes in, but the body's energy reserves will be so severely

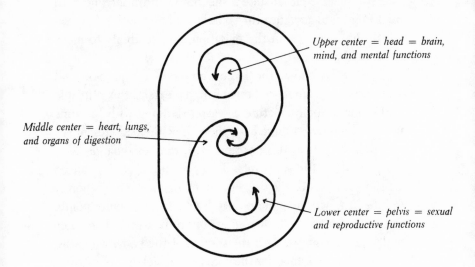

Upper center = head = brain, mind, and mental functions

Middle center = heart, lungs, and organs of digestion

Lower center = pelvis = sexual and reproductive functions

Figure 8.2. Energy centers of the body.

depleted that the end result may be death. The body's equilibrium may be altered momentarily—by holding the breath, for
example—but it must be restored if life is to continue.

The balance of opposing forces is inherent in the phenomenon of pulsation, which underlies life itself. Pulsation, which
describes a process of expansion and contraction, is apparent
in respiration, peristalsis, the beating of the heart, and other
bodily functions. It is basic to all living organisms, regardless
of size. In the case of the human body, it occurs not only in
the total organism but in every cell, tissue, and organ.

This model applies to behavior as well—the alternation between reaching out and withdrawal is a form of pulsation.
Reaching out leads to contact with the world outside one's self,
while withdrawal leads to contact with the self. This alternance
is influenced by the diurnal rhythm. We are more outgoing
during the day and more withdrawn into ourselves at night
when we sleep. Neither state is superior to the other, and both
are necessary to good health. To be stuck in either is pathological, for life depends on the pulsation, on the ability to move
out or withdraw as the situation requires.

Figure 8.3A shows the basic pulsation of expansion and
contraction in a single-cell organism. To extend this principle
to the human body, picture a person standing with his arms
and legs extended. Figure 8.3B shows how the body resembles
a six-pointed star in this position, with the head, hands, legs,
and genitals as the six points. Two concentric circles can be
superimposed on this figure, one touching all the outer points
and the other all the inner points. Each of the six outer points
represents major points of connection to the world. The outer
circle can be equated with the surface of the body, while the
inner circle could stand for the core from which impulses arise.
In the human organism, every expansive impulse charges each
of the six points equally, just as every contraction withdraws

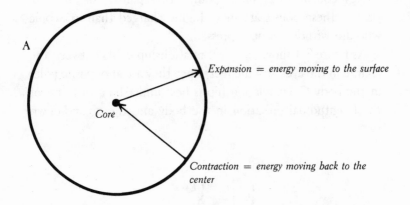

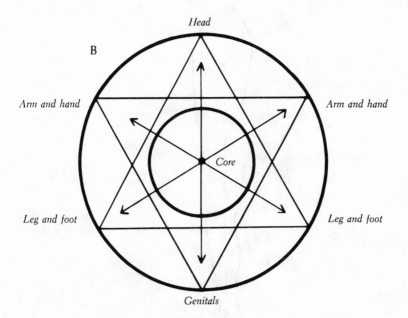

Figure 8.3. Expansion and contraction in the body.
(A) Basic pulsation in a single-cell organism.
(B) Basic pulsations in humans.

The Spirituality of the Body

energy equally from all six points. In expansive or outgoing people, these points are more highly charged than in people who are withdrawn or depressed.

As figure 8.4 shows, a direct relationship exists between the charge in the eyes and the feet, since they are at opposite poles in the body. That relationship is best understood in terms of the longitudinal pulsation in the body and the up-and-down

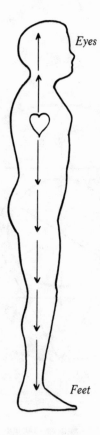

Figure 8.4. The longitudinal flow of excitation in the body.

flow of excitation. The body structure of all higher organisms is based on that of the worm, a tube within a tube, and composed of segments, or metameres. The inner tube consists of the respiratory and alimentary system. The outer tube functions as the voluntary muscular system. A worm moves when waves of excitation traverse its body, causing expansion and contraction in successive segments. The movement of food through the inner tube of the worm's body follows the same pattern. A similar principle applies to the human body, except that the body's structure is more complex and differentiated. In the course of evolution, various segments fused to form three major segments—the head, the thorax, and the pelvis—and two minor ones, the neck and the waist. Fusion has allowed these segments to evolve the highly specialized structures found to some extent in the lower vertebrates and to a greater extent in mammals. Evidence of the basic segmental structure exists in the spine, but even here some segments, notably S-1–S-5, have fused to form the sacrum.

The major segments are designed to protect the vulnerable organs within them. The thorax, the body's central segment, contains the heart and lungs, the two most vital organs, within the ribs' bony cage. The head, of course, contains not only the nose, mouth and eyes but the brain, which regulates the whole body from within the confines of the skull. At the other end of the body is the pelvis, a bony structure containing the organs of reproduction and elimination. The neck and waist, meanwhile, are largely passageways from one major section to another. Nerves and blood vessels pass through them, as do respiratory and alimentary tubes. Figure 8.5 illustrates these different segments of the body. These passageways provide the possibility of flexion and rotation. The degree of movement possible between segments depends on the length of these connecting parts.

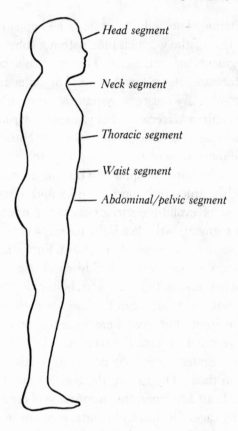

Head segment

Neck segment

Thoracic segment

Waist segment

Abdominal/pelvic segment

Figure 8.5. The segments of the body.

Let us examine some of the problems that can arise from distortions of this structural dynamic.

When a connecting segment is elongated, it distances the two major structures it connects, indicating a degree of separation between them. Thus, the elongated neck puts the head well above the body. A person with such a neck is likely to hold himself superior to his animal nature. He may look refined, but all he has succeeded in doing is to cultivate his feelings so that they meet cultural standards. Individuals with short necks and heavier bodies are likely to be closer to their animal nature and more identified with the brute strength of the body. Of course, genetic factors play an important role in determining body structure. But as we have seen in chapter 1, environmental influences also play a role in shaping the body's form. In particular, parental demands and attitudes have a great impact on a young child's body.

Some years ago I worked with a young man who was exceptionally tall and thin, with a sensitive face and beautiful curly hair. I could easily imagine him as a golden-haired boy. His mother had raised him with the idea that he was superior to other boys. He was God's gift to her, she felt, and she saw in him certain godlike qualities. The effect of this was to distance him from the earth so that he was not grounded. While his legs looked strong, they had little feeling in them. Nor was he strongly connected to reality, because he saw himself as special. Although he had some artistic ability, he could not achieve any prominence as an artist. He also had difficulty with women, because each woman represented to him his powerful mother.

The question is, what caused this young man's body to elongate in this fashion, especially given the fact that his father had a more normal build. I believe we can understand his development in terms of the body's longitudinal pulsation. In the long, thin body, the wave of excitation is drawn upward, reducing its intensity. This upward movement can have several meanings: a reaching up for affection and support, as a child reaches to be picked up; a withdrawal from one's basic animal nature; and a drive to rise above others. Grounding exercises reversed this direction, bringing more energy into his legs and feet, which helped this young man overcome his hang-up of being special. While this treatment did not make him any shorter, it did make him feel more solid and secure. By learning to breathe more deeply, he also increased his energy and strengthened the energetic pulsation throughout his body, which helped him feel stronger and fuller.

If a long, thin body represents the weakening of the energetic pulsation, a short, thick body represents the strengthening of the same pulsation, since compressing a wave increases its power. Individuals with this build have considerable physical strength. Prone to pushing their way ahead, men with this build often look and act like bulls. Nikita Khrushchev had this kind of build, together with an aggressive personality. But such a build can also be associated with an attitude of passive resistance, as in the case of Arnold, a man in his late forties who consulted me because of anxiety.

Although Arnold had never done any vigorous exercise, he resembled a weight lifter, with immense, rippled muscles. In talking with him, I quickly ascertained that his problem with anxiety stemmed from his relationship with his mother. Arnold was an only child. His mother was an aggressive woman whose main interest in life was her son. Not surprisingly, he experienced her as invasive, possessive, and controlling. When he was a child, his strongest desire was to get away from her. Unfortunately, his father was no help in his struggle to be free. Arnold was still struggling to escape his mother's clutches when he came to see me. He did not gain his freedom from her on an emotional level until she died when he was about fifty years old. By that time he had married for the first time, but he felt as trapped with his wife as he had with his mother.

As Arnold described his mother to me in the course of our work, I began to conceive of her as a tank and of him as a pillbox. In the struggle of a tank against a pillbox, neither can win. Because the pillbox cannot be crushed, it can effectively resist the tank, but it cannot destroy the tank. Nor can it run away. Similarly, Arnold could not escape from his mother, though he could—and did—resist her. The therapeutic problem was to change the pillbox into a fighting machine, which could be done by mobilizing the held-in anger. But one had to go slowly. Arnold was terrified of his anger because it had a murderous quality. His anxiety stemmed from the conflict between his desire to act upon that feeling and his fear of doing so. He felt that if his anger exploded it would destroy him as well as others. He had to protect himself with a defense that was as powerful as the force it had to contain. When Arnold understood the dynamics of his structure and his problem, it became possible to release the held-in anger safely by having him hit the bed regularly and under control. Keeping him grounded prevented him from flying off out of control and injuring someone. Slowly, his body relaxed; surprisingly, it also became taller.

In describing Arnold and his mother in this fashion, I am suggesting an essential aspect of their personalities, which was reflected in the structural dynamics of their bodies. The correlation between body and personality is absolute because of the functional identity between them. The body is not simply a vehicle for the mind, with the mind a separate force acting upon it. Instead, spirit is inherent in the living tissue. In death, the spirit is extinguished, and the body becomes pure matter. The spirit is like a flame that transforms matter into energy. The fire itself is not substance or energy but the process of transformation. When that process stops, the flame disappears, and the matter subsides into dead ashes.

Structural dynamics enable us to understand the phenomenon of splitting, a major disturbance in the body that can be correlated with an equally significant disturbance in the personality. The idea that people can have split personalities is not new. Some individuals have even been described as having multiple personalities. According to the above thesis, these splits must exist in the body to the same degree that they exist in the personality. Such splitting is possible because the human body, as we have seen, is divided into three major segments; the head, the thorax, and the pelvis. Splits between these segments occur when the feeling of connection is lost between them. There are many people whose heads are not connected to their hearts and whose hearts are not connected to their genitals. In all these cases, one finds tensions in the muscles of the neck and waist that limit the flow of excitation between the major segments. Of course, on a deep level, these segments continue to be connected. The nerves from the brain, which regulates and coordinates the vital functions of all segments, pass freely from one segment to another. So do the blood vessels, which carry oxygen and nutrients to every cell of the body and carry waste products away. This organismic integrity is reflected in a similar integrity at the unconscious level of the personality. On the surface, however, where consciousness resides, the integrity is broken by the disruption of the excitatory wave, which flows along the surface. Depending on the severity of the disruption, the break can result in three different patterns of behavior, each associated with one of the major segments. This is illustrated in the following case:

Some years ago, I was consulted by a man in his late forties, whom I will call Roger. Roger complained that he felt depressed because he was losing control of his life. He was aware that he was drinking too much, eating poorly, and neglecting his body. He was also on the verge of losing his wife. He attributed some of his problems to the fact that he often traveled on business. More often than not, he would visit a bar or a disco, meet a woman, and end the evening by spending the night with her. Roger had no difficulty picking up women, since he was a handsome, successful, charming man. But his relationship with his wife was deteriorating, and he suspected she was on to him, especially since their sexual life had dried up. Roger said that his wife was a good-looking woman but that she didn't attract him anymore. However, he was reluctant to end the marriage because they had three children to whom he was attached.

I saw that Roger had a very sharp and logical mind, which no doubt accounted for his success. But he spoke with very little feeling, and his eyes were generally cold and dark. It would seem that he had a good grip on himself, but his apparent self-possession was belied by his behavior. I realized that he could stay in control as long as he operated only from his head. Throughout the first months of therapy Roger showed very little emotion when discussing his past or present life. Yet there was something appealing about him. On occasion he would look at me and smile. At the same time a beautiful light would come into his eyes, and for a moment he would look like a bright-eyed, innocent child. When the light faded out, his eyes became dark. Sometimes they would light up again when he talked about his feelings for his mother and for other women, and a strange excitement would seem to possess him. He recognized that women fascinated him and admitted that he had been involved with several women other than his wife during the years of his marriage.

To help Roger, I had to understand who he was, but this was not easy. By day he was a cold, logical engineer and a successful businessman. By night he was a satyr. At rare moments he became a bright-eyed, innocent child. This side of his personality was responsible for the creativity he showed in his work and for the charm he exerted on women. Once I recognized the three-way split in his personality, I was able to understand its basis in his body, which was also split in three parts: namely, the head segment, the thoracic segment, and the pelvic segment. Severe tensions in the neck and especially at the base of the skull effectively cut off the head from the rest of the body. Similar tensions in the waist and around the pelvis isolated the genitals from the heart and the head.

The cold, professional side of Roger operated solely from his head. In that role his eyes were without any expression at all. The wildly passionate side of Roger operated solely from his genitals. In that role Roger lit up with an unholy fire. One doesn't expect a person to be cold and logical in the heat of sexual passion, but a normal person doesn't lose his reason when these feelings are aroused, as Roger did. As I pointed out in chapter 6, the loss of the ego and the surrender of the self ideally occurs only at the height of orgasm. In such instances, the surrender of the self operates to fulfill the self. In contrast, the surrender of the self to sex without love is self-destructive. I believed that Roger was capable of love, and that belief enabled us to work together to resolve his problem. But when we first started out, he was incapable of connecting either his thinking or his sexual desire to love. Because of the splits in his personality, he could not unite these different functions.

As I pointed out in chapter 1, a person's life experiences structure his body, which in turn shapes his personality. It is in this fashion that his past lives on in his present. For an individual to be freed from the restrictions of the past he must become aware of the experiences that imposed these restrictions in the first place. That is the task of analysis, which provides a framework within which restructuring can take place. Restructuring requires direct work with the body to reduce muscular tensions. Both analysis and restructuring should proceed hand in hand. I generally start with the patient's history, which at the outset is invariably incomplete. In the course of therapy a clearer picture emerges as repressed memories rise to consciousness.

Roger was an only child. He described his mother as an attractive woman wrapped up in her appearance and her social position. She liked entertaining and going to parties. His father was a hardworking businessman who often came home late from the office. His parents seldom fought, but he sensed that the relationship between them was not a happy one. Roger felt close to his mother but knew that her interest in him varied. When his father wasn't home, she would turn to him for companionship, sometimes complaining about his father's insensitivity to her needs. But when there was a social event on her calendar, she ignored him. Roger had a few pleasurable memories of playing ball and occasionally fishing with his father. Although Roger was rarely hit or punished by his father, he realized that his father was an angry man. In the course of the therapy, he became aware that as a child he had been frightened of him.

So far there is very little in this history to explain the severe disturbance in Roger's personality. But Roger's true relationship with his mother is only hinted at. When a woman is unfulfilled in her marriage, she is likely to turn to her son for the closeness and affection she does not receive from her husband. In many ways Roger had been his mother's confidant. But whenever she had the occasion to go out or to meet other men, she turned away from him. A similar betrayal occurred every night, when she closed the door to the bedroom she shared with his father. When I pointed this out to Roger, he realized that he had felt betrayed. I felt obliged to explore this part of Roger's history carefully, because it was clear to me that Roger treated women as his mother had treated him. He could be charming and intimate in a superficial way, but he could not give himself fully to any woman. He was sexually seductive with them, as his mother had been with him. Underlying this behavior was an intense anger, which was a transference of the rage he felt against his mother. Harboring such rage forced Roger to cut off his heart feelings from his sexual feelings, a split that was reflected in the lack of connection between his thorax and his pelvis.

Unfortunately, Roger also had to cut off his feelings of love for his father. As a child he had been caught in the oedipal triangle. Favored by his mother, he had been vulnerable to the jealousy and hostility of his father, who was the stronger, more powerful male. Roger stated during his consultation that he was not aware of having been afraid of his father as a child. But it eventually became clear that he had suppressed his fear, just as he had suppressed his anger against his mother for her seductiveness. That fear emerged later, as his repression lifted. He realized then that he had become more successful than his father in order to outdo him. But he achieved this success only by keeping a tight control over his need for love and understanding. Success on these terms was a meaningless achievement that left his life empty of feeling. He was driven to drink and to sexual acting out to break the control his head exerted. This in turn allowed some feeling to flow in his body.

Caught in the intense oedipal conflict of childhood, Roger had split apart. But a core of integrity remained that brought him to therapy to undertake a search for his true self. That self was revealed every so often in the bright, innocent eyes of the child within him. When I saw that look, I realized that Roger had been the object of both parents' love as an infant and young child. Swept up in the adult passions of the oedipal conflict, he had abandoned that child, locking it in his heart. Roger wanted to open his heart but could not do so except in those rare moments when he felt hopeful that someone would understand his confusion and his fear. It was his fear of surrendering to his feelings—fear, anger, sadness, love—that was manifested in the splitting of his bodily integrity.

The therapy of a split personality like Roger is not easy. Analyzing behavior, though essential, is not an effective integrating force because it primarily engages the mind. Roger recognized the validity of my interpretations, but that had little effect on his feelings or his behavior. Emotions, being whole body feelings, have the potential to integrate the personality. But how can one mobilize an emotion that is strong enough to have this effect? And which emotion would that be? Only two emotions have this power: love and anger. The only person who can evoke these emotions in the strength necessary to integrate the personality is the therapist. I became the father whose love Roger wanted, and I was also the father of whom he was afraid and toward whom he would have an anger proportional to his fear.

The projection on the therapist of the suppressed feelings of childhood is known as transference. All psychoanalysts work with this aspect of the therapeutic problem, but mainly on an intellectual level. Generally, that is not good enough to change a patient's psychological and physical structure. The transference must be experienced vividly. This was not easy with Roger because he was ambivalent about me. He needed a father's support and love but also felt superior to his father. He recognized my authority as a bioenergetic therapist and cooperated in the body work of breathing, grounding, and expressing some feeling. But he always remained in control with his mind and could therefore not give in fully to me, to the therapy, or to himself and his passion.

Roger was also afraid of me, though not physically, for he was younger and stronger than I. But he felt, and to some extent believed, that I, like his father, had power over him stemming from the fact that he needed my help. His need for help made him feel submissive, which, given the oedipal situation of his childhood, evoked the unconscious fear of castration. To become angry with me, on the other hand, increased the risk that I would reject him by terminating the therapy. He also wanted my love, as he had wanted his father's love, so he tried to impress me by working with his body doing the bioenergetic exercises. But this activity was handicapped by his ambivalent feelings. While the exercises made him feel better, he could not give in fully to them because he resented the need to impress me. It was an impossible situation, and after several years of effort, it seemed that the therapy was headed for failure.

But it is precisely at this point that the therapy has a real chance to succeed. If one accepts failure, one has nothing to lose. One can therefore be true to one's self. At this point, then, Roger was able to express his full anger toward me and his father. He did this by hitting the bed with his fists and saying how much he resented my attitude of superiority. The anger quickly transferred to his father for not being there as a man to support him by dealing openly and directly with the conflicts in his relationship with his wife. The words he used were "You are not a man." The meaning was that his father lacked integrity. He was also furious with his mother for her betrayal of his love and her lack of integrity. The release of this anger took place over a period of time, in the course of which Roger gained a feeling of integrity that allowed his love to flow.

Roger's therapy took a number of years, but he did not complain about the time, for he sensed that it was moving in the right direction. He could feel the progressive change in his body as he got more in touch with it through his feelings. The changes in his body were also reflected in corresponding changes in his behavior and his relationships. He was able to feel a deep love for his wife, and they found a fulfilling pleasure in their renewed sexual contact. But his sexual behavior changed radically. For a time, as he improved, he lost his sexual drive. This upset him until I pointed out that he had simply given up his sexual compulsivity. Sex would now be more an expression of love, which cannot be programmed or scheduled.

A classic female example of a divided self is Marilyn Monroe. Monroe was never a patient of mine, and I know her only from her movies and photographs, but her body shows a disturbance similar to Roger's; namely, the lack of a strong, unitary flow of energy connecting the head to the chest and the chest to the pelvis. In Monroe, each of these segments of the body seems to move independently, much as they would in a doll with a swiveling head and hips. This lack of connection between her body segments was also manifested in her public persona and behavior. Monroe was a very competent actress, a child and a sex queen, each personality functioning in a different situation. When she was acting, her behavior was controlled by an intelligent and competent mind. In her relationships with men, she was like a child needing approval and affection. To the public, she was a sophisticated and highly sexual woman. The reality belied the image. Marilyn Monroe was not an integrated person with a solid and secure sense of self. She had been traumatized as a child by the lack of love and by sexual abuse.

As we discussed in chapter 6, nothing destroys the integrity of a child's personality so much as sexual abuse, which can range from sodomy and incest to an emotional seduction between parent and child. For Monroe, this negative environment resulted in a severe energetic contraction in her body, similar to the pinching effect cold has upon a plant, which split the unity of her personality. I shall return to this subject in the last chapter.

The personality is vulnerable to the process of splitting because of the conflict between the rational mind and the animal body, between the drive to dominate and the need to belong.

This conflict is inherent in human nature. While it leaves man vulnerable to illness, it is also the source of his creativity and the basis for his conscious spirituality. The outcome in any individual's life depends on how severe the conflict is and how deep the split goes. It also depends on how well the society in which he finds himself handles its own split between culture and nature. Transposed into the family arena, society's split becomes a war—between husband and wife and parents and children. In this situation the child is often split asunder.

As we discussed briefly in chapter 5, if the conflict is not too severe and the opposing forces not too powerful, the child can hold on to some integrity by rigidifying his body. Usually the rigidity affects the neck and the waist. In most cases, the rigidity is not so severe that it becomes a medical problem, though it may cause problems that in time will require medical intervention. A loss of flexibility in the neck can lead to arthritic conditions in the vertebrae that make it painful to rotate the head. Similar tension in the area of the waist will affect the lumbar vertebrae, often resulting in lumbosacral pain, sciatic involvement, and slipped or ruptured disks. It is important to see this rigidity as a defensive posture. The individual is saying in body language, "No, you cannot break me or split me." Unfortunately, the rigidity develops after the child has already experienced some degree of being broken or split. The rigidity acts like a splint, preventing a small break from becoming a complete split.

However, the integrity that rigidity provides is based on immobility rather than flow, on will rather than feeling. Rigidity, in effect, is a statement of negation rather than of affirmation. It says, "I won't yield, I won't soften, I won't give in." Originally directed against social or parental demands and threats, once it becomes structured into the body, it becomes a resistance to life. By restricting the flow of excitation through the body, it interferes with pulsation and limits respiration, which decreases the energy level. But since it serves a survival function, people often regard it as an asset rather than a liability. This is especially true in those cases where a person is unaware of his rigidity until it leads to pain.

Since the ego controls the voluntary musculature, rigidity is an expression of the will. Its statement is "I won't," which could also be "I will." "I won't submit" could be equally stated as "I will overcome." Rigid people have strong wills, but this is not a sign of health. The will allows a person to achieve, but it does not permit him to enjoy, because the latter depends on the ability to yield. In itself, the will is not unhealthy or neurotic. In an emergency it can be lifesaving, as it was originally for the rigid person. It takes on a neurotic aspect when it becomes structured in the body to the extent that the person cannot surrender it to give in fully to his heart or his sexual passions. Despite the seeming integrity rigidity provides, the individual is split between his head and his body, between thinking and feeling.

In effect, we are dealing with a quantitative factor. Every individual in our culture suffers from some degree of splitting. When not severe, this splitting is accompanied by rigidity. A severe degree of splitting results in a visible break between the major segments of the body. To the degree an individual is split, he is robbed of his grace and denied the spiritual experience of identification with the universal. For just as the will separates the head from the body, it separates the individual from the community of his fellow men.

On the other hand, separateness allows individuality to flourish. It is because he has a will that man can be an individual. But having a will and being willful are two different things. Stiffening in an emergency is quite different from being stiff all the time. Yet we value rigidity in our culture because it produces a driving force. Speaking broadly, we are a driven people. We think it is great to achieve, to succeed, to overcome, never realizing that there is nothing to overcome in life but our fear of life itself. The more afraid we are, the more rigid we become.

Here is an exercise that tests for rigidity by gauging the amount of flexibility in the neck and the waist:

EXERCISE 8.1

Stand in the basic position described in the preceding chapter. Look over your left shoulder, turning your head to the left as far as it will go. Hold this position for several breaths and try to feel the tension in the muscles running from the base of the skull to the shoulders. Turn your head to the right and look over your right shoulder while breathing deeply for several breaths.

This is an exercise that I perform every morning as part of my personal-fitness program. I do it five to ten times on each side.

To gauge the flexibility of the waist, lift the arms with bent elbows to shoulder height and extend them sideways. Now twist your body to the left as far as you can and hold this position for several breaths. Next twist to the right and hold this position for several breaths. Can you feel how much tension you have in the muscles of the back and waist? While doing these exercises, are you able to breathe into your lower abdomen? Are you standing in the correct position: feet parallel, knees slightly bent, weight forward?

True rigidity involves the whole back, which can become almost boardlike from head to sacrum. I once knew a man who suffered from an ankylosing spondylitis, an arthritic condition of the back so severe that the vertebrae became a solid column—a very extreme example of rigidity. This man could not bend or turn his body, and his attitude was as stiff as his back. His father, I knew, was a very successful and dominating person who demanded complete obedience from his son. On the surface, the boy was obedient, but inwardly he stiffened in resistance. Unfortunately, he suppressed his feeling of resistance to the point where it became structured in his body. This man could not even mourn the tragedy of his illness, for to cry is to yield and soften, which was impossible for him.

Generally, tension in the muscles of the back is associated with suppressed anger (see fig. 8.6). In anger the wave of excitation flows up the back and into the teeth (for biting) and the arms (for hitting). When an animal is angry, its back rises, and the hair on it stands erect. When a person is angry, his back also rises. We say of him that he has his back up, which indicates that he is ready to attack. Expressing the anger discharges the excitation and allows the back to drop down again. However, if the anger is suppressed, the tension persists and becomes chronic. Such a situation is established in childhood when a child first feels an attack upon his integrity, generally when a parent commands him to do something he doesn't want to do. If his resistance to the demand is met with punishment, the child's natural response is to become angry. Unfortunately, his anger may be met with a punishment severe enough to force him to suppress his anger. In that case, he will yield, but only on the surface. Inwardly he will stiffen in resistance, holding back the expression of anger but not surrendering the impulse, which stays alive in the unconscious. As an adult, he may not feel the anger he harbors, but it is present in the rigidity and tension of his back, which he can't see because it is behind him. Even if he could see the unnatural curvature of

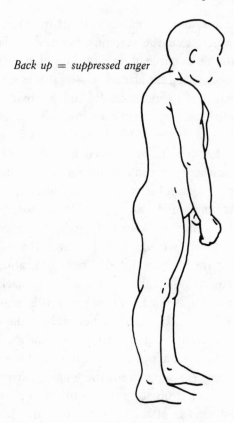

Back up = suppressed anger

Figure 8.6. The chronic tension of suppressed anger.

his upper back, he would not know how to interpret it, which is the task of therapy.

The rigidity of the back cannot be significantly reduced until the suppressed anger is made conscious and discharged. A person might become dimly aware of his underlying anger if he finds himself subject to uncontrolled outbursts of rage or plagued by a constant feeling of irritability. However, since such responses are unrelated to the original cause, they are ineffective in discharging the tension. Only when that tension becomes alive can one feel the anger and connect it to the traumas that caused it.

As I mentioned in chapter 5, the basic exercise I use in bioenergetic therapy to help release tension in the back is hitting a bed with one's fists or with a tennis racket. No one is hurt in this exercise, which is an effective way to discharge the chronic tension of held-in anger. I use the exercise in the therapy room and also recommend that patients do it at home. It is advisable that the bed have a foam rubber mattress to take such abuse. Men generally use their fists, while women use a tennis racket to feel more effective.

EXERCISE 8.2

Face the bed, standing with the feet apart and parallel. The knees should be bent to provide springiness, since the movement comes from the ground. Raise the fists or the tennis racket over the head, leaning back slightly. Do not bend too far back or you will break your connection to the ground. Instead, to gain power, pull the arms back as far as possible, keeping them close to the head. This may be difficult because of tension in the shoulders, but with continued practice the tension will dissipate.

With the arms poised, take a deep breath and strike the bed. Try to make the movement start in the feet so that the action is graceful. Since there is less power in a forced blow, do not attempt to hit the bed as hard as possible. As in archery, where the distance an arrow flies depends on the extent to which the bow string is drawn back, the strength of any muscular action depends on the length of the stretch, not on the intensity of the contraction.

Be sure to breathe deeply and freely. Do not hold the breath.
The exercise may arouse strong feelings of anger, but that is not
its objective. The blow itself is an expression of anger. It will
release the tension in the back if done properly over time.

It is best to do the exercise regularly, giving the bed twenty
to fifty blows each time.

I myself have performed the exercise many times to help me
release the anger I hold in my back. I had been aware that my
back was up, rounded, and constricted. One time while getting
a massage, I explained to the masseur, as he worked on my
back, the reason for the tension, which I identified as held-back
anger. Then I spontaneously said, "I don't have to be angry
anymore." As I made this statement, I had the sensation of
something dropping in my back. I felt straighter and freer, as
if a burden had lifted. I had let go of some of the rigidity and
control restricting my life.

To let go of control, the head must give in to the body. How
difficult that is for most people in the industrialized world! Too
many of us live in our heads and not in our bodies. How to stop
the incessant activity of our conscious mind is a subject I will
discuss in a later chapter. First we need to understand some of
the functions associated with the head, that part of our body
with which we face the world.

9

Face to the World

THE face, consisting of the mouth, the nose, the eyes, and the ears, is the part of the body most exposed to the external world. Used to signal feelings and attitudes, it is also the most expressive part of the body. It virtually broadcasts what we are feeling to the world unless we are determined to keep our feelings under wraps. Even then, a trained eye can detect a counterfeit expression. For example, I have never seen a happy person who was real. More often than not, a person with a happy face is trying to mask feelings of sadness. I have known some people who were at peace and had some pleasure in their lives, but they neither considered themselves happy nor wore a smiling face.

I once had a patient who considered himself a happy man and who said that his friends saw him that way, too. When I asked him to drop the smile he customarily wore, his face

assumed a very sad expression. It was obvious to me that his
happy face was meant to cover his sadness. It was not difficult
to discover the reason why. When the patient was a child, his
mother was depressed, and it was his job to cheer her up. Now,
as a man in his fifties, he used the same happy face to keep his
own spirits up.

The fixed smile is the most common mask people wear. It
covers feelings of sadness, anger, and fear and identifies the
individual as a "nice" person. But it is only a facade. In private,
the person who wears a smiling face may reveal quite another
side to his personality. For this reason, a fixed smile is always
to be distrusted. When I encounter it in a patient, I try to make
him conscious of it so that he can get in touch with his true
feelings. Otherwise, his personality is split; the ego identifies
with the smiling face, while the body responds to the patient's
innermost feelings. Such a split not only disrupts the integrity
of the personality but also robs the body of its gracefulness and
threatens its health. By keeping painful feelings buried in the
body, one places an enormous stress on the internal organs.
The person who denies the long-standing sadness and anger
associated with the early loss of love, for example, is particularly
vulnerable to heart disease.[1]

In my opinion, cancer is another illness that is closely related
to the suppression of feeling. I have seen a number of cancer
patients who in the face of this often fatal illness smiled and
expressed their confidence that they would overcome it. In one
case in which the condition was clearly terminal, the person
still smiled and insisted that he would recover. But one cannot
fight for health when one is split off from one's feelings. The
despair that underlies many cancer cases erodes a person's
energy unless it is brought to the surface and expressed.[2]

Another mask I often see is that of the clown or buffoon.
This mask also depends on a smile, but it expresses a different

attitude—namely, that the situation the person is in is not serious even when it is. This attitude may be expressed broadly—in clowning around, for example, or in a chronically sardonic half smile. It occurs in people whose parents hurt and humiliated them. As children, they learned to save face at almost any cost. They denied being crushed because to admit their feelings would have amounted to a surrender of their sense of self.

Saving face is, or has been, a very important consideration for Oriental people. Many go to considerable extremes not to allow their feelings to be seen, for to do so would entail a loss of social position. Like Westerners, Orientals wear masks, but they are not intended to disguise feelings by projecting their opposite. The Oriental mask has a placid, emotionless expression because Oriental philosophy extols a life of contemplation undisturbed by the tides of passion. Eastern religions ask adherents to calm the body, not to rise above it. The idea is to quiet the body so that one can sense the pulsation at the core of one's being that unites one to the universe. Just as still waters run deep, so a quiet person feels deeply. In the Orient, an expressionless face is regarded as the correct way to face the world. Since this attitude is ingrained in childhood, it becomes structured in the body so that it is difficult for an Oriental to express feelings or even to allow them to show. Children naturally imitate their parents, adopting the same bodily attitudes and facial expressions. But because such masking does not entail a split in the personality, it leaves gracefulness intact. Grace is important in Oriental life, but it does not carry an ego charge. Being graceful has always been the natural way, the Tao. However, I doubt whether this attitude will continue in the face of increasing industrialization.

It is the eyes that inevitably reveal the difference between a genuine smile and a mask. A genuine smile is the result of

a wave of excitation that flows upward, brightening the face
and lighting up the eyes, just as a house lights up when someone is home. Vacant eyes give the impression that a person's
house is empty. The emptiest eyes of all are those of a dead
person. I once looked into the eyes of a patient and saw the
empty look of death. I was sure that the person had died a long
time ago, not physically but emotionally. I have also seen a
vacant look in the eyes of schizophrenics, whose minds are
elsewhere and whose eyes do not make contact.

When I was a medical student studying ophthalmology, I
opened my textbook to find the statement "The eyes are the
mirrors of the soul." I was excited by the prospect of learning
more about this aspect of the eyes, but the words "mirror" and
"soul" were never mentioned again. Science is interested only
in the mechanical functioning of the organs, not in their inherent spirituality. If something cannot be measured, it cannot be
dealt with scientifically. We have no way to measure soulful-
ness objectively, or love or hate. Yet we have all been regarded
by loving eyes, hateful eyes, and soulful eyes. We know beyond
the shadow of a doubt that all these intangible qualities exist.

Perhaps it would be more correct to think of the eyes not
as mirrors but as windows through which we look at the world
but also through which we are seen. Like the windows of a
house, our eyes are equipped with shutters and shades. When
we close our lids, we not only shut out the world, but we can
dim the inner light that would also serve to hide us from
peering eyes. This became very clear to me in the course of my
work with a retarded young man, whom I will call David. David
was about twenty-three years old when his mother brought him
in for a consultation. I had never treated retardation before, so
I was reluctant to undertake his therapy. But I was curious
about David's condition, so I decided to look into his eyes. As
he lay on a bed, I bent over him, my face about ten inches from

his. I asked him to look at my eyes. As he did so, I exerted a slight pressure with my two thumbs just alongside his nose. David's face wore what could be described as an "idiot grin," but this pressure on the risorius muscles prevented him from smiling. To my surprise, I saw a look of intelligence flicker in his eyes. When he saw that I had seen it, his face resumed its previous expression, as if to say, "It's not true. I am not intelligent." But we had connected on some deep level. All the same, I did not think I could help him. I told his mother that I would refer him to a fellow bioenergetic therapist who was also an accredited child psychiatrist. David reacted strongly to this suggestion. Turning to his mother, he said, "Mama, mama, I want to work with Dr. Lowen." I was so touched that I could not bring myself to deny his request. I saw David regularly about once a week for four years.

In the course of his therapy, David made significant progress. However, I never once saw the look of intelligence on his face again. He had buried that aspect of his personality and was not prepared to bring it to the surface. It had only appeared during our initial consultation because he had been caught off guard. I wondered whether David was brain damaged, as his mother believed, or not. She said that he first showed some signs of retardation when he was about one year old. She attributed his condition to the shock of witnessing a violent altercation between his parents in which his father had struck his mother. His behavior in almost every respect had to be characterized as retarded, but he was able to take care of all his basic needs. Emotionally he behaved like a child of four or five. He seemed to know what was going on, but he would repeat himself and look to me for confirmation. He was also awkward in his movements. I noticed this particularly when we would shake hands as he entered each session. He would take my hand, but he would make no effort to clasp it. In response to my suggestion that he hold my hand more tightly, he would contract his shoulder. It took considerable work to get him to feel the ability in his hands to make meaningful contact with another person. He was able to hold objects—for example, he learned to play golf—but human contact was impossible. The wave of excitation necessary for such an action stopped at his shoulders and did not flow into his hands. In the same way, the light of his being did not show in his eyes. He was retarded, but he was also withdrawn. I felt he needed to come out as a person.

To do that, David needed to learn to assert himself. He was dependent on his mother, who controlled him. One of the exercises I used in his treatment was to have him lie on a bed with his legs extended so that he could kick them in protest. I asked him to say, "No," as loudly as he could at the same time. David seemed to love this exercise. He would say, "No," with glee and look to me for approval. It was obvious to me that it was very difficult for him to say, "No," to his mother. However, he had a rebellious side to his nature that came out in devious ways. For example, when he was out for a walk alone, he would set off the fire-alarm signal at one of the fire boxes on his way and watch the engines come tearing up to the box to learn where the fire was. Because he looked so innocent, the firemen never asked him what had happened even though he was the only person there. I was not aware of the other ways he expressed his rebelliousness, but I am sure he found many opportunities to do so.

Although his mother indulged him in many of his desires— not only did he take golf lessons from the pro at the club, but he had regular massages and wore fine clothes—his strongest desire was to have a job where he could meet other people. This his mother resisted until I insisted it was what he needed. He did find a job he loved in the shipping department of a company nearby, but it lasted only a matter of months. He wanted to get another job, but his mother made no effort to help him. However, he did improve with therapy. He was more alert, spoke up more easily, and moved more freely. Although he never mentioned an interest in girls, I could sense it was there, and I suggested to his mother that he take dancing lessons. I explained to her that the dancing would greatly improve his coordination and would give him an opportunity to hold a girl in his arms. His mother could easily have afforded the expense, but she did nothing to carry the program through. It seemed that she clearly had David's interests at heart—from the time he was a child she had taken him to specialists for diagnosis and treatment—but a short time after I suggested the dancing lessons to her, she canceled the rest of David's appointments with me on some pretext.

It was at this point that I realized what David's problem was. His mother needed him; taking care of him gave her life meaning. She had no real relationship with her husband, who she believed was involved with one of the women from his plant. Without David her life would be empty. How could she let him become a man and get involved with another woman? I never confronted his mother with my thoughts on this matter, certain that she would feel hurt and betrayed. Although the therapy ended on a note of failure, both David and his mother have kept in touch with me over the years. He calls me occasionally and expresses a desire to see me, but she never brings him in. Nothing has changed in their relationship. Having lost his personhood and his manhood, David now needs his mother as much as she needs him.

I believe this analysis explains David's retardation. He may have experienced some brain damage by neglecting his intellect, but I don't see that as the cause of his trouble. His mother sank her claws into him when he was young, and his only defense was to withdraw. He cut off his awareness of the situation to survive.

If we could look deeply enough into people's eyes, we would see their fears, their pain, their sadness, their anger—their every feeling. But these are feelings people do not want to expose. Especially in the East, but even in the West, to be seen as sad, frightened, or angry is to lose face. We try to hide our weaknesses from others and from ourselves. I believe we function according to an unspoken agreement: "I won't look into your soul if you won't look into mine." We regard it as a matter of politeness not to penetrate the masks people wear. As a result, we rarely *see* people. When people greet each other, they seldom look into each other's eyes. In response to "How are you?" they routinely respond, "I'm fine." How different this is from the traditional African greeting "I see you," which the writer Laurens van der Post has described.[3]

Eye contact is not only a form of recognition but also a way to establish an energetic connection with another person. We literally touch each other with our eyes. This is due to the fact that when eyes are charged, they project an energetic beam. People who are sensitive to the aura about the human body can actually see this beam, while others can feel it as a physical sensation. Many individuals have reported sensing that they were being looked at even though their back was to the person. If the beam between two people's eyes is tender and affectionate, it can awaken a feeling of love in their hearts. This is the basis for the expression "love at first sight." I myself have been touched by eyes that sent a wave of pleasurable excitement through my body. But just as eyes can radiate love, they can radiate anger and hate. We speak of the "evil eye," which is supposed to be able to cast a spell on someone. An angry look can be so strong that it can stop a person in his tracks. A hateful look can be powerful enough to freeze a vulnerable individual.

Our spirit shows and radiates from our eyes, which are the

most direct avenue for the expression of the body's spirituality. Eyes that are wide open, soft, and charged with the excitement of love express a high degree of spirituality. Such eyes see the world with wonder and awe. Unfortunately, too few people have such eyes. The world of their childhood was not an environment that would evoke such feelings. I am not referring to the physical world in which they grow up but to the quality of the emotional environment—specifically, to the relationship between the child and its parents.

Nothing determines the relationship between a mother and child as much as the quality of eye contact between them. When a child sees pleasure and love in his mother's eyes, he relaxes in a glow of contentment. My work with patients and my observation of people tell me that not many of our children have had the good fortune to see love in their mother's eyes. If a mother is depressed, her sad, empty eyes will become a cloud over the child. If she has any tendency to insanity, the look in her eyes will undermine the child's security and sense of reality. In this case, the child's vision may remain intact, but his eyes will become empty as energy is withdrawn from the surface of his body.

We shrink from pain, psychologically and physically. We do not want to see painful or unpleasant expressions or scenes. If this unwillingness to see becomes chronic and unconscious, it can disturb the eye's visual functioning. Myopia is literally an inability to see beyond one's nose. The myopic eye is a frightened eye, but the myopic individual rarely feels his fear. Nonetheless, his is a fear that dates back to childhood—a fear of seeing a look of hatred or anger in a parent's eyes. It is particularly devastating for a child to see a look of hostility directed against him in his mother's eyes. In an instant, the child's body contracts with fear, and he screws his own eyes shut so as to shut out his mother's face. In time, the child's chronic squint is structured in his body. The squint is an attempt to deny the reality of the vision of hostility. By narrowing the field of vision, it eliminates the threat. But if hostility from the mother persists, this defensive attitude breaks down, and the eyes become wide with fear. Myopia generally occurs just before the onset of puberty and, in my view, can often be associated with sexual anxiety. The connection of myopia with sexuality was confirmed by the experience of a patient who reported that whenever the downward wave of excitation reached her genitals her vision immediately improved. The flow downward is followed by a flow of excitation of the same strength upward into the eyes. They relaxed and became more alive.

The therapeutic task is to bring feeling back into the eyes. This means getting the myopic individual to sense the fear in his eyes and the person whose eyes are blank or empty to make contact with the eyes of another person, such as a therapist. I encourage my patients to look into my eyes; in most cases, I will bring my face close to theirs, as I did with David. In this way they can see into my eyes just as I can see into theirs. Most people tell me that my eyes are clear, and many tell me that they can see sadness in them, which I know is there. With the myopic person I mobilize an angry look in my eyes to evoke the fear in theirs. When feeling is expressed through the eyes, vision always improves. The grounding exercises also help by increasing the energy flow not only down to the feet but up to the eyes. However, this improvement will not last unless a significant change occurs in the personality, enabling the person to see himself and his life more clearly.

Eye contact is almost impossible when a person wears glasses. For this reason, I always ask my patients to take off their glasses so that I can look into their eyes. Many are reluctant to do so because they cannot see my face clearly. But focusing their eyes on my face helps their vision. I also move my chair closer to them to make the task easier.

Glasses not only prevent eye contact but shut out light. The Bates method for improving vision in myopic people emphasizes opening the eyes to light. One of the techniques involves visualizing a sunlit beach where the light is intense. The bright light of the sun counteracts the dark looks in the mother's eyes that originally forced the child to shut down his vision. By seeing the world as bright again, the muscles of the eyes relax. I discovered as much at the age of fourteen, when I was told I needed glasses. I got them, but I did not want to wear them, so I carried them in my briefcase. By the end of the week I had lost them. My mother had another pair made, which I lost as well. Although the glasses cost only seven dollars, my mother could not afford another pair. I read and studied in direct sunlight without them. I also played a lot of tennis on clay courts, where the light was strong. My eyes steadily improved. Surprisingly, since that time I have never needed glasses to see or read. At the age of seventy-seven, I can still function without them, perhaps because I have a need to see and to understand in life and in work. I tend to be farsighted, which is also a trait in my personality. All in all, I am visually oriented, a fact that may have other roots, such as a frustrated sexual curiosity in childhood. Whatever the reason, I am thankful that my eyes are still alive.

Both the mouth and jaw are connected to the eyes by way of the energetic pathway in the front of the body. Significant tension in the jaw muscles reduces the charge in the eyes and lessens visual acuity, as the following exercise shows:

EXERCISE 9.1

Thrust the jaw forward and tighten the jaw muscles as much as you can. Do you sense a change in your visual acuity? Do

objects seem less clear? Do you have some trouble focusing?
The tension in the jaw prevents the body's excitation from
flowing into the eyes.

Some years ago I was consulted by a woman who had had
a breast removed for cancer. Lois was about fifty years old,
married, and the mother of grown children. She entered my
office wearing dark-tinted glasses. When I asked her to take
them off, she replied that she would not be able to see me
without them. She was extremely myopic. In addition, her lips
were thin and narrow, her expression was tight-lipped, and the
set of her jaw could only be characterized as grim. Lois insisted
that her childhood had been a happy one and that she had a
good marriage. But her body strongly contradicted this statement. Her eyes were wide with fright, which she was clearly
determined to overcome, and her face expressed a disapproval
of frivolity and pleasure. When she was a child, her father had
expected her to be strong, successful, and secure, and as a result
she became determined never to be afraid or sad. She grew up
to become a successful businesswoman, hardworking, shrewd,
and above all, determined. When she came to see me, she was
determined to overcome her illness by willpower, but this was
a fight she could not win. She had to feel her fear and see what
she was afraid of. If she could, the energy she used to squelch
her feelings would become available to her immune system in
its fight against the disease.

We all set our jaws when we are determined. In most cases,
the tension dissipates when the need to exert the will is past.
Any chronic tension in the jaw reflects a chronically determined personality. In Lois's case, we saw that fear and sadness
were responsible. In reality, determination cannot overcome

fear. One may suppress fear so that one doesn't feel afraid, but the fear lives on in the defense against it, as in Lois's case. Of course, there are situations in which one should not give in to fear, as in a fire, when it is essential not to panic. But here the exercise of the will is conscious. This is not the case when determination is characterologically structured in the body.

The determination not to be afraid is more than a mental exercise. The jaw must be set to prevent feelings of fear from becoming conscious. Sadness can also be suppressed by tightening the jaw. After all, one cannot break down into sobs unless the jaw is loose enough to quiver.

It is the inability of most parents to tolerate their child's crying that forms the basis for a determined attitude later in life. Initially parents may make some effort to quiet a crying child, but if the crying persists, they may become angry enough to threaten or strike him. It is as if the child's crying drives them crazy and must be stopped at any cost. In such circumstances, a child suppresses his crying. He may grow up into an adult who can still shed some tears, but he will find deep sobbing almost impossible. Unfortunately, by suppressing his crying, he also suppresses his ability to love. A tight jaw blocks feeling from flowing into the lips, which makes kissing an empty gesture.

A tight jaw may either protrude or recede. The protruded jaw denotes an aggressive attitude, one expressing a readiness to fight, and is often accompanied by clenched fists and an angry look. If the jaw is locked and immovable, the aggressive feeling is unconscious. The retracted jaw denotes the pulling back of any aggressive impulse. A person with such a jaw is sometimes characterized as weak chinned, a Milquetoast. He, too, is unaware that he is holding back any aggressive impulse. In either case, the person needs to free up his jaw so that it can move freely forward, back, and to the side. I urge patients in therapy to thrust their jaw forward as strongly as possible to sense the aggressive quality of this movement. If a person is suppressing anger, this gesture may help him get in touch with it. If the thrust of the jaw is strong enough, anger will also show in the face and eyes as energy flows into them. Generally, I suggest the exercise be accompanied by verbal statements. The person might say, "I hate you," or even, "I could kill you." At the same time, his fists should be clenched to engage the whole body in the expression of rage.

The strong thrust of the jaw also expresses defiance. In my experience, every patient needs to learn to express this attitude because very few are able to assert themselves openly and directly against a superior force. In childhood this superior force was a parent. In adult life it may be a spouse or an employer. Some patients are openly rebellious. Others are more covert. Their resistance takes the form of unconscious bodily rigidity—a subtle posture of "I won't." While they seem to go along with an order or request, they hold back inside and sabotage the result. The submissive personality and the rebel are really opposite sides of the same coin. Just as the rebel fights his own tendency to submit, the weak-willed person harbors an inner rebelliousness.

The following exercises are designed to release tension in the jaw muscles. Getting in touch with such tension, and with the feelings of anger or of murderous rage that underlie it, is a positive experience that gives one greater self-control.

EXERCISE 9.2

Stand in the basic standing position as described in the previous chapter. Thrust the lower jaw forward and hold it in this position for thirty seconds while breathing evenly. Do you feel some pain in the temperomandibular joint area? Are the muscles tight? Move the jaw to the right and the left, keeping it thrust forward. This movement may evoke further pain in the back of the neck. Now open your mouth as wide as possible and see if you can insert the three middle fingers of your hand between your teeth. In many people the tension in the jaw is so strong that they cannot open their mouth wide.

Let your jaw relax; then thrust it forward again, clench your fists, and say "I won't," several times in a forceful tone. Does your voice carry a sound of conviction? You can also try this exercise with the word *no.* In bioenergetic therapy the patient is encouraged to use his voice, to say "No" or "I won't" as loud as he can as a form of self-assertion. The more forceful the expression, the stronger the sense of self engendered by it.

The impulse to bite is the final aspect of tense jaw muscles that needs consideration. While nursing, infants often clamp down their gums on their mother's breast to help them suck efficiently. The teeth are also our first weapons of defense and attack. An infant is able to bite before it is able to strike a blow. All through childhood some children bite as an expression of anger. My own son at the age of four bit our Afghan hound to stop the dog from pushing him out of the way. For most parents, hitting is far more acceptable than biting, which many see as irrational and frighteningly animalistic. Biting the breast poses particular problems. It often occurs when a mother attempts to withdraw the breast before a child is finished nursing. In such a situation a baby's bite can be quite painful, but if his mother reacts angrily, the child may become afraid to bite. He will suppress the impulse by tensing his jaw muscles. I would say that every person who suffers from TMJ syndrome or from tense jaw muscles has suppressed biting impulses.

Releasing these impulses discharges tension and relaxes the jaw. Suppressing them weakens the teeth and is responsible for many dental problems.

Many years ago I treated a patient who had a recurrent dream of attempting to bite and feeling her teeth crumble in her mouth. When I met her, she was suffering from severe periodontal disease, and a number of her teeth had become loose as a result. She was under a dentist's care, but I could see that she needed to bring more energy into her teeth and face. She told me a story that she had heard from her mother, a sad tale that explained her dream.

When she was a baby, this patient recounted, her mother played a game with her. She would offer the child her breast but then withdraw it when the baby reached for it with her mouth. The mother found it very amusing to see the child's face pucker up as she began to cry, at which point the mother would offer the breast again, only to withdraw it one more time. The child eventually got the breast, but she was seriously traumatized by this game. The natural impulses of her mouth to reach out, take in, and hold became associated with anxiety and insecurity. One natural impulse was to bite the breast when it was offered to be sure of having it, but she sensed that such an action could mean the loss of the breast. She may have actually bitten the breast, which would have provoked a very angry reaction. My patient learned very early that to bite would have severe negative consequences and so she withdrew the energy from her teeth in fear and gave up any desire to bite. But that desire did not die, for biting is a part of the nature of the human animal. The exercise of that function was felt to be dangerous, as the dreams showed. Working this problem bioenergetically plus good dental care resulted in a significant improvement in her dental condition.

To sink the teeth into an object is to possess it, as every hunting animal knows. Patients need to feel their ability to bite and to appreciate the sense of power it gives them. One exercise I often ask them to perform is to bite on a rolled-up towel. I am always amazed by how many people are fearful of damaging their teeth. Sometimes I engage in a biting tug-of-war. Like two dogs tussling over a bone, each of us bites one end of a towel with our teeth and tries to pull it from the other. This exercise also mobilizes the neck muscles, which are contracted in many people. It poses little danger if one grips the towel firmly with the back teeth.

Of course, not every oral impulse is a hostile one. Babies reach out with their lips to nurse, and adults reach out with their lips to kiss. Yet many people find it difficult to reach out softly with their lips. When they attempt to do so, they thrust their jaw forward. As we have seen, this movement of the jaw expresses a negative attitude—"I won't"—which undercuts the positive gesture of reaching out softly with the lips to kiss. The thrust of the jaw says "I won't yield." This is typical of the ambivalence that characterizes the behavior of neurotic individuals. Part of them wants to reach out, another part holds back out of fear and anger. The net effect of the action is zero, an absence of any real feeling in the kiss. To experience the excitement and joy of life, one must be able to give in fully to one's longing and desire for closeness and contact. The ambivalence must be resolved. This cannot be done psychologically alone, since the ambivalence is structured in the muscle tensions about the mouth. Considerable practice is needed to mobilize the lips independently of the jaw if the reaching out with the lips is to be free and full. As the tension goes out of the muscles of the mouth, the lips will vibrate with excitement, just as the legs do in the grounding exercise. Patients then feel their lips in a new and alive way.

Most people have difficulty reaching out with the upper lip. They have been trained to keep a "stiff upper lip," which is equivalent to putting a lid on tender feelings. If one doesn't reach out, one can't be rejected and hurt. It is clear that such an individual was badly hurt as a child when in all innocence and with an open heart he reached out for contact (love). But the stiff upper lip also has another meaning. If one is hurt, one will not cry. It is almost an axiom in Western culture that crying is a sign of weakness. Some people pride themselves on their ability not to give in to their feelings of hurt and sadness. Even when faced with the loss of a loved one, many believe that it is a sign of strength not to cry. There can be occasions when it is advantageous not to break down and cry, but for this to be a healthy reaction it must be a conscious choice, not a structured attitude. If one can't cry, one can't rejoice.

Crying is like the rain: sometimes gentle, sometimes violent, but always essential to the life of the earth. Just as a land without rain becomes parched, a life without tears becomes a desert. If we can't cry, we cut ourselves off from other people. Many people are afraid that if they cry they will literally lose face. I have heard many women remark after crying deeply, "I must look a mess." It is true that their face is not pulled together, but often they look radiant nonetheless. The glow in their eyes and face looks like the sky after a rain: clean, bright, fresh, and sparkling.

After a storm passes, the newly washed sky is serene, and the world seems at peace. Unfortunately, however, in human beings, emotional storms rarely clear the air completely. The reason is that peace of mind depends on peace of body. A body at peace is not still; rather, its flow of excitation is like that of a big river—deep and full. Just as rocks in a river disturb the flow, causing turbulence, so chronic muscular tension in the body interrupts the flow of feeling, producing conflicts and emotional "noise." These disruptions make human beings the only creatures that lack peace of mind. How to regain it is the subject of our next chapter.

10

Peace of Mind

ON the physical level the conflict between the ego and the body results in a loss of grace. The same conflict also robs the individual of peace of mind. In most people, when they are awake, the mind is constantly active, with one thought following another, often without any discernible overall pattern. This flow of thoughts, or "stream of consciousness," is generally regarded as a positive attribute. Often, however, it reaches an exaggerated degree; the individual is preoccupied with thinking about himself and his problems and is, therefore, to some degree separated from his surroundings. The constant focus upon what is going on in the mind diminishes feeling contact with other people and with the environment; it undermines the spiritual sense and decreases the capacity to love; for love, like spirituality, depends on the ability to reach out beyond one's self. Not only does preoccupation cripple the ability to transcend the self, it also limits the individual's identification with his true self, which is the feeling state of his body. Without peace of mind, the fulfillment of being, which is manifested psychologically in an attitude of graciousness, becomes impossible.

In a few individuals with superior intelligence, such mental hyperactivity may produce some brilliant scientific theories. However, there are a number of reports of creative insights that arose spontaneously when the individual was not trying to think. In the average individual this constant mental activity revolves around personal problems for which in almost all cases there is no logical solution. Most problems stem from a conflict between feeling and thinking, between what one wants to do and what one thinks one should do. If we had faith in our feelings and followed them, as do animals, we would have peace of mind. But human beings are blessed or cursed with a mind that seeks to understand and control nature, including the body. Man is not god, however; his knowledge is limited and his understanding is imperfect. Believing that he knows and thinking that he is right, man turns against nature. It is a struggle he cannot win but one he is afraid to lose. As long as he struggles, as long as there is conflict in his personality, he cannot have peace of mind. Of course, the degree of conflict and the intensity of the struggle vary with different people. We must understand that peace of mind results from harmony within the self and with nature.

In chapter 2, I pointed out that it takes energy to relax. The reverse is equally true. If we don't quiet down, we cannot accumulate the energy reserves we need to meet the stresses of modern living. And to quiet down, we must fully inhabit our bodies. The more we do so, the less exclusively we rely on our conscious selves. It is a basic principle in bioenergetics that a person loses touch with any part of his body where chronic muscular tension exists. The more rigid his body is, the less feeling he has, and the more the body comes to resemble a machine. Simultaneously, the brain becomes more active, and the person begins to base his sense of self entirely on his thought processes. The body becomes little more than an apparatus to transport the head and to carry out its thoughts. There is very little life in such a person, and not much spirituality, either.

The rigid individual's life devolves into one long struggle to find a resolution to the inner conflicts he has. During the day, the brain is constantly churning; at night, the individual is subject to nearly continuous dreams. Dreams represent an unconscious effort to resolve and release the conflicts and tensions in the body. Although dream images occur in the brain, the whole body is involved in the act of dreaming. We know that dreaming is accompanied by rapid eye movements and sexual arousal. But it is also possible to talk, cry, or scream in a dream or even to strike or kick out in anger. During sleep, the ego's guard is down, which weakens its inhibitions. The tension fueling the dream may be the result of a recent experience or a repressed experience from childhood. It may also have its roots in the tension inherent in human nature—namely, the conflict between the knowing mind and the instinctual body, between individuality and identification, between control and faith.

Conflict has both a creative and a destructive potential. A debate between supporters of two opposing views might well lead to deeper understanding. A war between them, however, would have destructive consequences for both regardless of who wins. The ancient Chinese were well aware of the need for harmony between antithetical positions and opposing forces. Today, we might achieve such harmony by integrating Eastern and Western philosophies. The Western way to peace of mind is through the process known as analysis or therapy. The Eastern way is through meditation. I shall examine each in turn and show how they can be integrated.

At the outset it must be recognized that most therapeutic efforts fail to help the individual resolve his conflicts and find peace of mind. In my opinion, there are two basic reasons for this failure. One is a lack of understanding by the therapist of the nature of the problem, and the second, related to the first, is too great a dependence on insight to change behavior. Throughout this book I have emphasized that one needs to look at the body, to observe its movements and read its expression, to understand the individual and to evaluate and treat emotional disturbances. These disturbances are structured in the body and manifested in its loss of gracefulness. An analysis or therapy that focuses largely on the presenting complaint or symptom is not a holistic approach because it does not comprehend the whole individual. The goal of gracefulness cannot be achieved by working solely through the mind. It is a mistake to believe that deep emotional conflicts can be resolved through conscious reasoning alone. The far greater part of our actions and behavior is governed by feelings and impulses of which we may or may not be aware. Analysis attempts to bring these unconscious forces, threatening as they may be, to consciousness. Psychoanalysis depends largely on free association, slips of the tongue, the interpretation of dreams, and the analysis of transference to shed light on the unconscious. Jungian analysis relies more heavily on dream interpretation. But because such methods are indirect, in most cases they do not reach deep enough. Even if patients become aware of some of their unconscious motivations, such insight does not generally lead to significant change. Neurotic attitudes and behavior are largely structured in the body by chronic muscular tensions over which the mind has no control. These tensions have to be released before any real resolution of conflict can occur.

Bioenergetics is a more powerful and effective technique than analysis alone because it offers a more direct route to the unconscious. By reading the body's language, the therapist is able to see a patient's personality conflicts immediately in areas of rigidity and chronic tension. By working with the body as described in earlier chapters, the patient learns to sense these tensions and to get in touch directly with his unconscious. Such an approach does not neglect the use of verbal analysis, including the interpretation of dreams and the analysis of resistance and transference, but its primary focus is the body. Rigidity is softened, chronic tensions are released, and the body is freed to feel the life of the spirit. In effect the body recovers its natural gracefulness.

In most cases a person cannot accomplish this alone. Feelings that have been suppressed are generally too frightening to be experienced without the support and understanding of a therapist, who acts as a guide to the patient's unconscious. How good a guide he is depends on the extent to which he has explored the unknown world of his own unconscious. I like to compare the therapeutic experience with Dante's account of his adventures in the *Divine Comedy*. When the poet finds himself lost in a wood with three wild beasts ahead of him, he calls upon Beatrice, his protecter in heaven. Because the way home passes through hell and purgatory, Beatrice sends the Roman poet Virgil to guide him. As they traverse hell, Dante sees the punishments visited upon sinners. The passage is dangerous because a false step could leave him stuck in one of hell's pits. Only with Virgil's guidance does Dante make it safely through hell and purgatory. The patient in therapy goes through a similar experience on the path to self-knowledge and health. His own private hell consists of the painful feelings he suppresses in the interest of survival—despair, panic, rage, humiliation. The chronic muscular tensions these suppressed feelings cause cannot be fully released until the feelings are brought to consciousness and expressed. That process requires the help of a therapist who has traversed his own hell, learning its dangers and finding his own way out.

The great majority of modern people are suspended between heaven and hell, occasionally glimpsing each. We may experience moments of joy, but we sense all too often that we could fall into a pit. The only way out of this precarious situation is to do what Dante did. By exploring one's personal hell, by descending into the depths of one's being with the light of consciousness, hell is abolished, for hell can only exist in darkness. Similarly, when suppressed feelings are brought to consciousness and accepted, they can no longer torment us.

At a bioenergetic workshop, a patient of mine stood before the group of participants and screamed her hatred for her mother for not allowing her to be a person and for not being a person herself. Jane's mother never expressed any feeling and never allowed her daughter to express any, either. She was a submissive woman who put on a smiling face and pretended everything was fine. Jane's father was an unintelligent, uncouth, and closed-off individual who regarded all women, including his daughter, with disgust. An attractive woman in a doll-like way, Jane came to therapy complaining that her body was completely numb from head to toe. Although there was no organic disturbance, she had never known any sexual feelings. Her only desire was to be shown some kindness. But she dated men who used her and worked for employers who exploited her. She had every reason to be angry.

In the course of a long therapy, Jane slowly became alive. Her body regained feeling, she began to experience herself as more of a person, and she learned to stand up for herself. But at the time of the workshop, she still had not recovered her sexuality, though she did feel how deeply hurt she had been and how sad she was at the loss of so much of her life. As she screamed her hatred before the group, her face was contorted, her eyes were small, and her fists were clenched and shaking. She looked demonic. It was as if all the fury of hell were unleashed in her outburst. She said later that on some level she knew this hatred was inside her but she could not touch it because its intensity made her feel as if she were a monster. After she unleashed it, her face was soft and relaxed, and her eyes were bright. She felt freer.

We conceive of hell as a place deep within the bowels of the earth. Our personal hell is deep within the bowels of the body, in the pelvic cavity where our sexuality is fettered. Here lie the roots of our true spirituality, the base of the kundalini's current. Here in the womb is where life begins and where we first experience the bliss of paradise. When we are born into the world, we are expelled from paradise. We may recover that feeling of bliss when, safe in our mother's arms, we nurse at her breast. We may also know it when, secure in the love of our partner, we join with him or her in a sexual embrace. There may be other occasions when we experience the joy of fulfillment, but I believe it is conditioned upon our being in touch with this deep part of ourselves. We know we are in touch when we experience the wave of excitation flowing through our body to the pelvic floor and through our legs into the ground.

Eastern religions are well aware of the importance of getting out of one's head and descending into the depths of one's being. Meditation is the technique used to accomplish this. By quieting the mind's static, it allows us to hear the soul's sounds. Its rules are very simple. One finds a quiet corner where one will be free from the sounds and distractions of the outer world. Orientals generally adopt the lotus position or sit in a kneeling position on the floor. Westerners may prefer to sit on a chair. To quiet the mind, a mantra, or short prayer, is recited. One sound commonly used is "omm," which is like a loud hum. In transcendental meditation the person is given a short, individual statement. In my opinion the words are relatively unimportant. It is the sound of chanting them that has a quieting effect by preventing the vocal cords from forming words. It has been shown that the vocal cords are active while we think even though the words they shape are soundless. If the vocal cords are engaged in producing a sound, they cannot produce words at the same time.

However, it is not necessary to make a sound in order to meditate properly. The key to meditation is to breathe deeply, which helps one relax. But here we run up against the fact that it is impossible to relax chronic muscular tensions of which one is unaware. In most people these tensions need to be worked through analytically and physically to free the body from their grip. It has been my experience that meditation is easier and more effective for Orientals than it is for Westerners, who are tenser. However, to the degree that one can relax and breathe deeply, meditation helps in experiencing some peace of mind, as the following exercise shows:

EXERCISE 10.1

Find a quiet place. Sit on a hard chair in such a way that your feet are flat on the floor and parallel.

Hold your head up and sit as straight as you can. Feel your backside on the seat of the chair. Allow your arms to rest softly on your knees. Do not make yourself rigid, as this will defeat the purpose of the exercise.

Close your eyes and focus on your breathing without making any particular effort to breathe. You will become aware that breathing in and out happens by itself. You will feel the respiratory wave (the wave of excitation) as it passes through your body, flowing up as you breathe in and down as you breathe out. Stay focused on the wave, allowing it to flow deeper and deeper into your belly and pelvis. To accomplish this, you must relax the lower part of your body by letting your belly out and your buttocks drop. Most people hold up the pelvic floor, as we noted in an earlier chapter. Do you feel the respiratory wave flow all the way down to the pelvic floor?

Stay with this exercise for about ten minutes if you can. Keep your mind strongly focused on the in and out of your breathing so that you can sense the basic pulsation of your body. You may feel it through your whole body from your feet to your head. If you do, you may become momentarily aware that you are part of a pulsating universe. At that moment, you have stepped out of the self and into the universal.

I have a personal way of meditating that I have found very helpful. While walking, I focus my attention on my body to feel every movement that it makes. When I can let my legs carry me, I feel at one with my body, the ground, and the environment. My breathing becomes spontaneously deeper, extending into the pelvis. My mind stops forming words as it follows the sensations that arise in my body. I also use the same technique when I do my bioenergetic exercises. The principle is to feel the body, and the exercises are designed to accomplish this. It is a principle that can be applied to every activity.

One lives fully in the present when one fully inhabits one's body. Consciousness extends so deeply into the body that one feels the pulse of life. This is the way animals function. A cat lying in the sun and gazing out a window is a perfect picture of an organism at peace with itself and the world. We human beings experience that state when our present includes our past and determines our future, with tradition serving as the con-

necting link. Centuries ago, people lived in terms of mytholo-
gies that kept the past alive in the present and the future clearly
defined. But theirs was a horizontal culture in which there was
little growth or change. In a culture like ours, which is constantly changing, the connections between past, present, and
future are often broken. As the past is suppressed and forgotten, the future becomes dangerous and uncertain. In chapter
8 we saw the damaging effects on the personality when the
connections between the major segments of the body are disrupted. We are looking at the same problem here from a more
global perspective.

At our very core is an animal soul in harmony with nature,
with the world, and with the universe. If we are cut off from
it, our minds still function logically, but our thoughts have little
human value. As Saul Bellow wrote, "In the greatest confusion
there is still an open channel to the soul. It may be difficult to
find. . . . But the channel is always there, and it is our business
to keep it open, to have access to the deepest part of ourselves—to that part of us which is conscious of a higher consciousness."[1]

No such channel exists in the mind. Instead, it exists in the
body as the channel through which waves of excitation move
into the pelvis. Then, being pendular, the wave flows up as high
as it previously flowed down. A higher consciousness is connected to a deeper consciousness. A tree can reach up to
heaven only to the extent that its roots dig deep into the earth.
In the next chapter, we will look at that higher consciousness.

11
Love and Faith

THE statement that man cannot live by bread alone implies that a person needs faith as well as bread in order to survive. While bread alone would sustain the body, the human animal needs a different sustenance for his spirit. That spiritual nourishment is love, which is a deep, heartfelt connection to another person or persons, a different creature, nature, or God. I don't believe that human beings are unique in this need. The spirit of any animal will languish if that animal is isolated from contact with life. Many wild animals die when they are subjected to captivity because their spirit is broken. They were part of a certain environment; it sustained their bodies and gave meaning to their lives. That meaning lay in the excitement associated with the drives for food and a mating partner. I would characterize an animal's connection to its environment, including the creatures in it, as one of love on the same level as the love a person can feel for his home or his land. Some animals, such as geese and swans, that mate for life become so attached to a partner that its loss could lead to the death of the animal. Can one question the power of love or the devastating effect of its loss upon the individual?

What is the connection between love and faith? Does an animal have faith? The answer to the latter question depends on whether we are talking about faith as a belief system or as a bodily attitude. The distinction is very important because it is possible for an individual to proclaim his faith and yet act in such a way as to belie that assertion. In chapter 1, I discussed the case of Ruth, who made a seemingly remarkable recovery from a severe illness through her belief in the immortality of the soul and the healing power of Christian Science. That recovery, however, was not fully sustained, and so we may think that her belief wavered or weakened. It was not the belief that healed her but the surge of her spirit in response to the belief. We can also say that it is the intensity of the feeling behind the belief that is the effective force. The feeling can be love or faith, for both are positive and expansive impulses associated with a strong wave or state of excitation. Love is an effective healing force regardless of whom one loves. It is the act of loving that has the power to heal. In the same way it is not the content of the belief system that determines the power of faith. That power resides in the nature of faith itself.

If love is a bodily feeling and faith a bodily attitude, we can say that an animal is capable of feeling love and having faith. The attitude that characterizes its faith is its unconscious acceptance of the rightness of its world. That rightness is represented by the fact that the animal fits its environment almost as if they were made for each other. For the tiger there will be prey, for the beaver there will be water, and for the squirrel, a tree with nuts. We say that an animal is adapted to its environment, which means that it can count on its environment, secure in the understanding that it will not be betrayed. With this security an animal feels at ease in its natural environment. It has not fallen from grace.

That was man's condition in the early days of his existence, before he developed self-consciousness. At that time, his faith in nature and life was biologically determined by the full and free flow of excitation in his body. He belonged; he was a part of the natural order, and it was right. We also have God's word that it was right, for, according to the Bible, after he created the world, he looked at it and was pleased. In those days man's world was described as the Garden of Eden. But after man ate the fruit of the tree of knowledge, he was expelled from the Garden of Eden and forced to earn his food by the sweat of his brow. He became a tiller of the soil, and in that act he set himself apart from nature.

The development of agriculture did not lead to a complete break with nature or to a loss of faith. It did, however, introduce a new stage in man's relationship to the world. No longer was he just one of earth's creatures, all of whom were animated by a vital spirit that had to be respected; he was a different creature who was special and superior. He recognized, however, that he was still dependent on nature, on the earth to produce its fruit. He sensed the existence of a power greater than any he had known before whose favor he needed to sustain his life. This power could be wooed by sacrifice and offerings. The rites associated with this practice became the belief system that embodied his faith. The power became the gods and goddesses that he worshiped. Conceiving of them in his own form, which was natural, he felt an affinity with them. He, too, became godlike in that he had a creative power within himself. He would call that power his soul and see it as godlike and immortal. The great Western religions are based on this view of the universe. Religion is man's vehicle for faith, whether it is the animistic religion of primitive man or the complex religions of modern man.

It is interesting to note that the Eastern religions retain more of the animistic beliefs as part of their religious understanding than do the Western religions. The Buddhists, for example, see all creatures as partaking of the Buddha nature. The Taoists of China believe in the harmony of natural forces and emphasize the need on the individual level for that harmony. In the West, the process of industrialization has gone so far that it has undermined the faith of most people in the rightness of their world, in the existence of a beneficent force in the universe that would ensure their survival and well-being. Instead of faith, we in the Western world have placed our trust in science, representing the power of the human mind to overcome all the difficulties that beset us. Some believe that all we need is goodwill and enough money to do the job. But such trust in science is naive, for it rests upon the assumption that man can be superior to nature, that he can become a god himself, omnipotent and omniscient. Man even dreams that he can overcome old age and death itself someday. But this dream is unrealistic not only because man as a part of nature can never comprehend the whole—his knowledge is always limited—but also because it ignores the relationship between man and nature. A delusion of superiority vis-à-vis nature destroys the connectedness that gives life its meaning, its excitement, and its joy. It denies the spiritual nature of man.

It would be unrealistic on my part to ignore the fact that reason and science have added greatly to our lives. No civilized person would or could fully return to a primitive way of living. We would miss the beauty and the excitement that culture has added to life, and we would find it almost impossible to survive without the skills and tools that man has developed over the centuries. We could not survive on that early level because we have lost the sensitivity to and understanding of nature that primitive man had. But the choice need not be either extreme—a helpless dependence on nature or a sophisticated independence from nature. Rather, we need a proper balance and harmony between the opposing forces in our personality, between our rational mind and our animal body, between our aspiration to fly and our need to be rooted in the reality of our dependence on the earth from which we derive our nourishment and support.

In the East, along with the maintenance of more animistic beliefs, people also have more faith in the healing power of the body. A faith in the healing power of the body, of course, does not dismiss the help that an antibiotic can offer in fighting a severe infection; but the belief that faith can perform miracles is not without validity. In so many documented cases, faith has turned a fatal prognosis into a seemingly miraculous cure. Such miracles, however, are not due to mysterious forces from outside the body that can enter and cure illness. That is the way much of modern medicine operates; namely, by intervening with drugs or instruments. Faith operates from within, although it may be evoked by an experience of love. Opening one's self to God's love, for example, has a very positive effect on the body through its exciting and expansive effect. When someone establishes a connection with the universal, which is the same as feeling the love of God, his energy becomes so heightened that it floods his body, radiating outward in a state of joyous excitation. This outward radiation can be seen as a beautiful aura about the body. And since this excitation or energy is the source of life, it can sometimes overcome the destructive effects of illness.

It may be argued that faith doesn't always have this positive effect. That is not true if we conceive of faith as a bodily response to life. Opening one's self to life (and, by extension, to love) always increases the level of energy in the body and therefore always has a positive effect. Faith must be defined, therefore, as the state of being open and allowing the natural excitation to flow freely through the body.

We cannot close ourselves off to life and yet live. As long as we are alive, therefore, we have some faith in life and in a universe that is the source of life. Only in death is there a complete absence of faith. By the same token we cannot be completely closed off to love, for then our hearts would turn cold and stop beating. Unfortunately, many people are partially closed off to life and love because of betrayals in childhood that forced them to contract in their bodies, diminishing their energy and decreasing their faith. They developed chronic muscular tensions that can be compared to an armor in that while these tensions are designed to protect the individual against further injury, they do so by enclosing him in a semi-rigid shell. He is only partially open to life and is distrustful of any action that seeks to penetrate his defense and reach his heart. But it is his very defense that undermines his health and renders him vulnerable to illness.

If the free flow of excitation to the surface of the body is a positive expression, chronic tension that blocks or constricts this flow is a negative expression. If openness is a life-positive attitude, being closed off in any degree is a life-negative one. If softness is a quality associated with life and love, then chronic rigidity is the quality associated with death and hate. Hate makes a person cold and hard, just as death does. While these negative features are directly connected to traumas that the person has suffered in childhood, they are maintained in adulthood by a fear of letting go, of surrendering to the body, of giving up control.

The human mind is constantly active in its search for security. It is nature that most threatens man's security—man's own nature and the vicissitudes of the natural forces in his environment. Because man can never completely subdue nature, he is in a constant struggle with it. This struggle between man and nature, which is mirrored in the struggle between the ego and the body, robs man of the peace of mind he needs to experience the joy that life offers. Only little children and wild animals know this joy, which Dostoevsky described as God's gift. This struggle is more intense in neurotic individuals than in healthy ones. It often masquerades as a struggle for power, success, self-esteem, or love.

Deeply religious people are able to avoid this struggle because of their faith in God. If a person has faith that his life is in God's hands and whatever happens is God's will, then he need not struggle. He may not be happy, but by abandoning the idea that he can control life or nature, he will at least know some peace of mind. With the surrender of the ego's control, a person can give himself over to the joyful flow of life and feeling in his body. For a people whose culture is based on the mind's power, a religion that demands the ego's surrender acts as an antidote to the narcissism inherent in the culture.

Eastern religions do not have an anthropomorphic god who is omniscient and omnipotent. Peace of mind is linked in the East to accepting the idea of fate. Despite an individual's actions, life is not thought to be fully in his hands. Since one is powerless against fate, it is useless to struggle.

Whether one submits to God's will or to fate, one gives up striving to change the conditions of life. This runs contrary to the modern belief in progress. Of course, great strides have been made in providing more of the world's people with greater opportunities for individual expression and a higher level of material comfort. But greater peace of mind has not gone along with these improvements. Quite the contrary. People are more anxious, more depressed, and more insecure than ever before. This may seem contradictory, but in subduing nature we have severed our own roots. Helpful as progress is, we must recognize that the direction it takes is always up, away from the ground. In the undeveloped countries people rest by squatting. In our culture no one squats, and few people rest. Instead, we have given up walking to ride in automobiles, and we further distance ourselves from the ground by flying in planes. When we move into space, we leave the earth completely.

It is from the ground up that one builds an integrated personality, just as one erects a house by first laying the foundation. One cannot find security in any thought process dissociated from its roots in the body's feelings. It would follow, therefore, that no thought is right for a person unless it also feels right to his body. I had an experience not long ago that validated this concept for me. I awoke one morning with the sweetest feeling in my whole body that I had ever known. Then a thought flashed through my mind: If you are true to yourself, you are not afraid of death. I knew it was true because it felt so right. I recalled that I had seen the film *Platoon* the night before. I didn't remember dreaming about it, but I sensed that it had inspired the thought. In the film, the American soldiers kill not only the Vietnamese but each other in an attempt to deny their fear of death. Acknowledging and accepting that fear would have loosened its grip on them and made them more human. Many people have faced death without fear because being true to themselves was more important than living a lie. Being true to one's self means to know and accept all one's feelings.

I have described the problem of the modern individual as narcissism.[1] The narcissist does not trust his feelings, cannot accept himself, because he feels that who he is does not measure up to what he is expected to be. We of the modern world are engaged in a futile effort to be different, to be superior to nature. Unable to trust ourselves, we cannot trust others. Without trust or faith in ourselves, we cannot trust nature. In the end, as in the Vietnam War, we will destroy others and then ourselves.

The villain in the scenario is always the ego, with its need to control life. Of course, the ego is also a creative force, but it can become destructive when it is not grounded in the body, supported by faith in the body and in nature. Without this faith, we must control and inhibit our natural responses, and in that process we build up explosive pressures within our muscles and so are afraid to lose control. A person who has faith does not create explosive pressures that require suppression because of their destructive potential; he therefore has no fear of losing control. With faith in life, he can allow the free flow of his natural impulses, modifying them only to ensure that their expression is appropriate, as we will discuss in the next chapter. Then the loss of control, as it occurs in sexual orgasm, as it occurs in the Sufi dances, as it occurs in the practice of Zen, leads to joy and fulfillment—a sense of the spirituality of the body.

12

The Gracious Mind

AS we have discussed, faith in nature is the basis for animal existence, the essence of animal spirituality. Human spirituality is of a higher order in that it requires that the ego also be integrated into the process. When the ego is well integrated, we can achieve the state of graciousness—raising the level of animal spirituality to the human plane.

The relationship of the ego or mind to the body is complex. The very existence of the will implies that a person can act against the body's desires. Such an action is positive when a person is able to overcome his panic in a dangerous situation and save his life. It is negative when he courts danger unnecessarily and injures himself or loses his life. Having a will allows man to be creative or destructive, noble or base, divine or diabolical. For this reason all religions recognize that the human animal must choose between good and evil, right and wrong. Yet despite the fact that man long ago fell from grace, he is not a lost creature. He is lost only if he prefers wrong to right, evil to good. If he is committed to truth, decency, dignity, and graciousness, he will be in a position to achieve a very high degree of gracefulness, health, and spirituality.

All the same, the actual role that choice plays in human lives is difficult to ascertain. As members of society, we are forced to assume that individuals have a choice, or we would not be able to punish them for transgressing social laws. Yet when I analyze a patient's behavior in my practice, I invariably find that it has been determined by his childhood experiences, most of which were out of his control. No child chooses to fall from grace, nor does he lose his innocence through an error in judgment. Instead, he is led from a state where ignorance is bliss into social consciousness. Along the way, his parents and teachers instruct him in what is acceptable and what is not. If these rules of behavior are in accord with community practice, if they are not arbitrarily or harshly enforced, they do not seriously affect the child's personality. Because human beings are social creatures, most prefer to live and act by these rules even if they entail a loss of freedom.

Every religion aims at helping man reconcile himself to the inevitability of struggle. In monotheistic religions, the solution is to put one's welfare in the hands of God by surrendering one's egotism and one's belief in one's own power. The Oriental religions also advocate a surrender of egotism and power. In Hinduism and Buddhism the goal is to merge the individual self with the universal self by seeking identification with Brahman or Buddha. In Chinese philosophy the goal is to strike a balance between the two great forces of nature, the yin and the yang. In all religions, humility is a key element.

If one doesn't withdraw from the world, the path of good

deeds, righteous living, and moral behavior is the only other way to achieve peace of mind and a truly spiritual life. I have been using the term *graciousness* all along to describe the attitude that embraces these values. It is my intention in this chapter to reinforce the idea that there is a biological basis for this path. It has been my thesis that a person who is naturally gracious is also naturally graceful.

On the animal level, life is lived with unconscious integrity. Unconscious integrity means that the animal acts according to what feels right or pleasurable. That is also the way that young children live and function. But with the development of the ego and the knowledge of right and wrong social behavior as taught by the parents, one can no longer depend on unconscious integrity to guide one's actions. As a social creature one can't do whatever one feels like doing. Even in some animal societies the young are taught a code of behavior governing relations within the group to reduce conflict and promote cooperation. Human societies, which are so much more complex, need more developed codes for the same reason. Unconscious integrity must be supplemented, therefore, by conscious integrity—that is, by principles. But the principles one will adopt to guide his life must not violate the unconscious integrity of his body or he will be in serious trouble.

A gracious person is a person with principles; expediency does not govern his behavior. Instead, he is governed by a code of behavior that stems from an inner sense of what is right or wrong. His code may include the moral commandments that his society establishes when they are in accord with his own sense of propriety. For example, the commandments not to commit adultery, not to bear false witness against a neighbor, to honor thy father and mother that are embodied in the code of Moses feel right to most people. Similarly, the principle to be truthful accords strongly with one's sense of integrity. My teacher, Wilhelm Reich, once said to me, "Lowen, if you can't say the truth, don't say anything." It is a conscious choice we make when we elect not to profit by dishonesty, even though we can gain some advantage by deceit. We choose the truth because it promotes the integration of the ego and the body, of the conscious mind and the unconscious impulses.

An unprincipled person functions in terms of his current desires and immediate needs. This kind of functioning is typical of the narcissistic individual, who thinks only in terms of himself. It is also characteristic of infantile behavior. Unlike infants, most adults have the ability to defer gratification. When a child is hungry, he wants to eat immediately. As a result, he may take whatever food is available. An adult, on the other hand, can tolerate hunger until both the meal and the setting are to his satisfaction. As a result, greater pleasure is available to the adult who acts like one than to the adult who acts like a child.

The ability to defer gratification, or its corollary, the ability to tolerate pain or frustration, is a function of the ego. In an infant the ego has not developed to where it can function to contain feelings and impulses. This development occurs largely during the years three to six, when the personality becomes anchored in genitality. The same energetic pulsation that establishes genital primacy also establishes the hegemony of the ego. In the narcissistic individual this development is disrupted by the incestuous nature of the oedipal situation, which forces him to split off from his genital base. That split, as we have seen, breaks the integrity of the personality and cuts the ego off from its base in the body. Containment becomes difficult, if not impossible, with the consequence that principles cannot be established.

Principles act to increase the pleasure and satisfaction in life by restraining the impulse to find immediate satisfaction. As we have seen in the case of sex, satisfaction is greatest when the whole body or the whole person is sexually excited by another. Containing this initial excitation allows a deepening of the feeling. At its deepest point, the heart becomes involved and the feeling becomes one of love. This means that feeling love for one's partner is essential for full orgastic release. The same is true of every other activity. Only if one's heart is in it will it lead to a feeling of complete satisfaction and fulfillment.

But one's principles are also important in another respect. Take the case where a person is head over heels in love with the spouse of a friend. If he thinks a sexual liaison would hurt his friend, he will be unable to consummate the relationship. Engaging in sex in these circumstances would spoil the pleasure. One might well find reasons to justify such a sexual liaison. The marriage may be an unhappy one. Or one may claim that love should override all other considerations. But a principled person will act according to his principles; to do otherwise would simply *feel* wrong. A split would be engendered in his personality, with one part saying yes and another saying no. As we have seen, such a split destroys the integrity of the personality.

A lack of principles is evident in the man who is a "womanizer" and the woman who is promiscuous. In the latter case, sexual activity stems from a lack of feeling and is an attempt to become sexually alive. Women who have been promiscuous report that they ceased that behavior when they gained their own sexual feeling. A man who is constantly after women may believe that he is a sexually potent male, but the reverse is true. Because he cannot contain the excitement, he is not fulfilled in the sexual act and so is impelled to keep running after women in the vain hope of finding fulfillment through sex. The joy of sex is available only to those who are filled with love and share that love with a partner. It is not surprising that promiscuous people are seen as unprincipled.

In bioenergetics, integrity is a term used to describe the uninterrupted flow of excitation in the body from head to feet and back again. We saw earlier that this flow is interrupted in many people by tensions that separate the head from the thorax and the thorax from the pelvis. These splits, of course, are on the surface, not in the depths of the organism, where the heart is connected via the arteries and veins to all parts of the body. But a person subject to these tensions is not conscious of his essential unity. In the course of therapy, when the energetic flow is reestablished, such a person will often exclaim, "I feel connected all over." The principle of integrity is based on feeling "all of one piece." Without such unity, a person cannot *feel* the difference between right and wrong, although he may know it on a conscious level.

In some individuals, the loss of integrity is so severe that their behavior becomes unprincipled. "Anything goes" is the maxim under which they operate. Such people are described as narcissistic in the psychiatric literature.[1] In its more extreme form, this personality type is characterized by an absence of conscience that leads to behavior that is designated as psychopathic or sociopathic. The psychopath cannot distinguish truth from falsehood and will tell an obvious lie in the belief that it is the truth. The sociopath cannot distinguish right from wrong. These are both extreme types, but some degree of splitting affects the integrity of all narcissistic individuals.

Narcissism is the most common affliction of modern man. The narcissistic individual lives behind a facade designed to earn him acceptance and admiration on the one hand and to compensate and deny inner feelings of inferiority, inadequacy, sadness, and despair on the other. A good example of this type of individual is the man who builds his muscles to project an image of manliness, strength, and power. In most cases, this macho facade hides a lost, frightened child. The split between the muscleman's outer appearance and his lonely inner feelings splits the integrity of his personality.

However, narcissism is not like a disease that one either has or doesn't have. In a culture like ours, which is largely oriented toward such ego values as power and success, most people have some measure of narcissism in their personalities. The real issue, then, is the extent to which one is in touch with his core feelings and his body. The more in touch we are, the more integrity we have.

From the above discussion, it should be clear that teaching moral principles in an educational setting has little efficacy. Principles have to be based on feelings that cannot be taught. In my opinion, moral teaching even in the home has value only to the extent that the parents themselves embody these principles and act upon them in their relations with a child. We cannot teach love, honesty, respect, dignity, or any virtue by words and not example. And we cannot teach integrity if we ignore the fact that it is a body phenomenon that is manifested in how one stands, moves, and behaves. We need to realize that the mind is not that potent—that no amount of preaching will enable people who are blind to see the truth. A more accurate statement would say that no amount of teaching will enable an individual to feel the rightness or wrongness of his actions if his body lacks integrity because it is split by tensions. The belief in the power of the mind fully to control behavior is the product of a mind that is not fully connected to the body and its feelings.

And yet it is necessary to formulate and teach ethical principles by which human beings can guide their behavior. To be effective, however, such teaching must recognize the basic role that the body and its feelings have in all issues of morality. This requires an emphasis upon the fact that moral behavior is designed to promote the good feelings of the individual as well as the welfare of the community. If a major goal of life is to be a graceful and gracious person, as I believe, then that must also be the goal of our educational programs, not the acquisition of knowledge. We must not be reduced into believing that knowledge and the power it offers can lead to the "good" life. The failure to live by principles that embody high ethical standards entails the loss of the greatest gift life has to offer—joy. Without integrity, physically and psychologically, one cannot know the deep pleasure and good feelings that come from moving gracefully, or experience the spiritual ecstasy of being a gracious person. Without these qualities, no matter how powerful or wealthy one is, one lives in a dark prison of fear, distrust, and enmity.

It is not easy to resist the appeal of power or the drive of desire. All of us yield occasionally and betray the trust placed in us. Unfortunately, this can happen even in the relationship between therapist and client, when the client is a desperate woman, the therapist an unfulfilled man, and both are unconsciously looking for love. In the intimacy of the situation, where one party opens her heart to the other, sexual passions are sometimes aroused that lead to sexual involvement. Almost all therapists subscribe to a code of ethics that regards such behavior as unprofessional and unethical. Even though the client is a consenting adult, it is the therapist's responsibility to protect her against any action on his part that would violate her trust and damage the therapeutic relationship. This is a moral principle that every therapist must honor regardless of his feelings. None of us can rely on feelings alone, because we cannot know whether an action is right or wrong until after the deed is done. Nor can we rely on reason alone, because the devil can persuade us as well as God. Reason and feeling must be united in principles that guide us in the proper and healthy conduct of our lives.

To have principles and to adhere to them is in a person's self-interest. But it can also be a supremely spiritual act. Human beings can emulate God's love for man by the love they show one another. God is not only omniscient; he is omnipresent. He is in all of us. Religious mystics of many faiths have written that God lives in the human heart.[2] When we feel the love in our heart, we are in communion with God. When we show that love, we often succeed in connecting with our fellow man. A gracious smile can uplift another's heart like a ray of sunshine. A gracious act can excite the spirit and open the soul to the beauty of life. The gracious person accepts others not as a matter of obligation but as a matter of love. This does not mean he never becomes angry but that his anger is like God's, direct and short-lived. After such a storm, the sky is clean and clear, and the sun shines brightly.

The soul is the name we give to the energetic system that animates every organism. If we are hateful, the heart contracts and the soul shrinks. If we are gracious, the heart expands and the soul swells. The radiance of a gracious smile comes from a heart filled with good feeling. The warmth of a gracious person stems from his intense passion for life and his lack of rigidity. One can't be gracious and driven at the same time. A gracious person is patient enough to make a sincere and warm connection with all those who come in contact with him.

The gracious person also has the sense that he is subject to something larger and more powerful than himself. I am referring, of course, to God and to the faith we discussed in chapter 11. Without such a force, what is there to curb man's egotism and greed, which sees the earth and its inhabitants as things to be exploited for one's personal desires and satisfactions? By yielding to his greed, man destroys the very ground upon which his own existence depends. We are all familiar with the pollution of the air, the earth, and the waters, with the loss of forests and the extinction of numerous species of wild creatures. Accompanying this destructive activity has been a breakdown of moral values and a corresponding deterioration in people's health and vitality. Depression has become endemic, and many people have felt the need to turn to drugs of one kind or another in order to carry on.

In the West, life has grown increasingly secularized. The sacred has been reduced until it exists only as a set of beliefs and symbols. These still have considerable power over some people's lives. But beliefs and symbols are mental processes that do not take the body into account. In the Western world view, the body falls into the category of the secular, the profane, and the material. This enforces the split between mind and body, which I have shown to be at the root of man's emotional distress.

It has been my intention in this book to show that the body is not simply a material object easily understandable in purely physical terms. No, the body is not a vessel for the spirit but the spirit made flesh. As we have seen, spirit resides in protoplasm, where it is made manifest in the ability of an organism to respond to its environment in a way that furthers its life process. This has been the story of life on earth for several billion years.

In my view, it is the mind, with its emphasis on knowledge and reason, that is secular and the body that is sacred. Much as we think we can explain the body's operations, at their core is the mystery of love. The heart of man, where love resides, is also the temple where God resides in the human being.

The basis for this belief is the ability to feel a resonance between the pulse of the heart and the pulse of the universe. While the pulse of life occurs in every cell and every organ of the body, it is felt most powerfully in the beating of the heart and experienced most vividly in the feeling of love. I have described the living organism as a state of contained excitement, with the heart as its center. That excitement crests and overflows the boundary of the organism when one is in love, at which time one senses one's connection to the universe. Love is the true spiritual feeling. I trust that most of my readers have experienced this feeling sometime in their lives.

But why only sometimes? The surprising answer is that we don't love ourselves enough. Self-love doesn't mean self-adoration, which is narcissism, a state that lacks the excitation of love. To love one's self is to be full of the excitement of life and to be responsive to that excitement in all its myriad manifestations. To love one's self is to love life and all living things. One can't fully love another unless one loves one's self. Without self-love one is a taker, not a giver.

With self-love, we can achieve the three forms of grace that Aldous Huxley once defined, as mentioned in the preface to this book—animal grace, the integrity maintained by the full and free flow of excitation in the body; human grace, through living the principle "To thine own self be true" and by extending this principle to our fellow men through gracious behavior; and spiritual grace, through connection to a higher order. Only through the integration of the personality on these three levels can we attain the transcendence that we call "the state of grace"—truly, the spirituality of the body.

Notes

Preface

1. Aldous Huxley, *The Perennial Philosophy* (New York: Harper & Row, 1945), 89–91.
2. Ibid., 166.
3. Ibid., 269.
4. Joseph Campbell, *The Power of Myth* (New York: Simon & Schuster, 1988), 199.

Chapter 1

1. Alexander Lowen, *Depression and the Body: The Biological Basis of Faith and Reality* (New York: Penguin, 1973).
2. This case is fully reported in Alexander Lowen, *The Language of the Body* (New York: Macmillan, 1971).

3. See Alexander Lowen, *Fear of Life* (New York: Macmillan, 1981), for a further discussion of the important changes that occur in one's life at this stage.

Chapter 2

1. Selva Yesudian and Elisabeth Haich, *Yoga and Health* (New York: Harper & Row, 1953), 21.
2. Herman Kanz, *The Martial Spirit* (Woodstock, N.Y.: The Overlook Press, 1977), 42.
3. See Wilhelm Reich, *The Function of the Orgasm* (New York: Orgone Institute Press, 1934), 326–29, for a fuller report on these experiments.
4. Ibid., 338.
5. William E. Seifriz, lecture and film at the University of Pennsylvania, 1954.
6. See Alexander Lowen, *Depression and the Body: The Biological Basis of Faith and Reality* (New York: Penguin, 1973), for a full analysis of the cause and treatment of depression.
7. Meyer Friedman and Ray H. Rosenman, *Type A Behavior and Your Heart* (New York: Fawcett, 1981); Alexander Lowen, *Love, Sex, and Your Heart* (New York: Macmillan, 1988), 110–14, 159–60.

Chapter 3

1. See Alexander Lowen and Leslie Lowen, *The Way to Vibrant Health* (New York: Harper & Row, 1977), 101ff., for a full discussion and illustration of these exercises.
2. See Alexander Lowen, *Love, Sex, and Your Heart* (New York: Macmillan, 1988), 83, 86.
3. See Alexander Lowen, *Bioenergetics* (New York: Penguin, 1976), 17–18.
4. Eugene Harrigel, *Zen and the Art of Archery* (New York: Vintage, 1971), 58, 84.
5. Margaritha Ribble, *The Rights of Infants* (New York: Columbia University Press, 1965), 82.
6. See Lowen and Lowen, *The Way to Vibrant Health,* for a full description and uses of the bioenergetic stool.

Chapter 4

1. See Stanley Keleman, *Emotional Anatomy: The Structure of Experience* (Berkeley, Calif.: Center Press, 1985), 107; Alexander Lowen, *The Language of the Body* (New York: Macmillan, 1971), 346–47.

Chapter 5

1. See Alexander Lowen, *Love, Sex, and Your Heart* (New York: Macmillan, 1988).
2. See Alexander Lowen and Leslie Lowen, *The Way to Vibrant Health* (New York: Harper & Row, 1977), 34, and Alexander Lowen, *Love, Sex, and Your Heart* (New York: Macmillan, 1988), 190.
3. See Alexander Lowen, *Pleasure: A Creative Approach to Life* (New York: Penguin, 1975), 187–93.
4. See Alexander Lowen, "A Psychosomatic Illness," *Bioenergetic Analysis* 2(1986): 1–11.

Chapter 6

1. See Alexander Lowen, *Narcissism: Denial of the True Self* (New York: Macmillan, 1985), 105–9.

Chapter 7

1. Alexander Lowen and Leslie Lowen, *The Way to Vibrant Health* (New York: Harper & Row, 1977), 11–12.
2. Lee Strasberg, *A Dream of Passion* (Boston: Little, Brown, 1987), 17.

Chapter 8

1. Wilhelm Reich, *Cosmic Superimposition* (Rangeley, Me.: Orgone Institute Press, 1951).

Chapter 9

1. See Alexander Lowen, *Love, Sex, and Your Heart* (New York, Macmillan, 1988).
2. See Wilhelm Reich, *The Cancer Biopathy* (New York: Farrar, Straus & Giroux, 1973).
3. Laurens van der Post, *A Story Like the Wind* (New York: William Morrow, 1972), 44.

Chapter 10

1. Saul Bellow, foreword to Allan Bloom, *The Closing of the American Mind* (New York: Simon & Schuster, 1987), 16.

Chapter 11

1. See Alexander Lowen, *Narcissism: Denial of the True Self* (New York: Macmillan, 1985), for a full discussion of this problem.

Chapter 12

1. See Alexander Lowen, *Narcissism: Denial of the True Self* (New York: Macmillan, 1985).
2. See Alexander Lowen, *Love, Sex, and Your Heart* (New York: Macmillan, 1988), 3–4, 208.

Index